THE ULTIMATE
MANDOLIN
SONGBOOK

26 FAVORITE SONGS ARRANGED BY JANET DAVIS

ISBN 978-1-4234-2241-9

Visit Hal Leonard Online at
www.halleonard.com

TABLE OF CONTENTS

The songs appear in this book in alphabetical order. These reflect a wide variety of musical genre and styles. Most songs will include a variation for each level player.

NOTE: The first version is arranged in the traditional style with emphasis on the melody. The next version(s) build on this.

ABOUT THE AUDIO

The audio for the *Ultimate Mandolin Songbook* include all of the songs played on the mandolin by Janet Davis at a moderate tempo. These are recorded in stereo, with the mandolin on the left channel and a MIDI band on the right channel. Both are normally heard at the same time, but a student also has the option to listen only to the mandolin without the band, or to hear only the band for playing along. Also, different versions for the same tune are played at slightly different tempos in order to provide a choice of tempos with which to play along.

The audio tracks are listed beside each song in the Table of Contents in the book. Also, the specific track number is indicated to the right of the song title and version number for each song throughout the book.

The 88 tracks include all of the versions for each song, except for a very few, which are almost identical to a prior version.

NOTE: In order to be able to include all of the songs and the different variations, the alternate licks are not included on the audio. Also, for the same reason, a song may be played without the repeats (this is noted with the track number beside the title).

NOTE: For more enjoyable listening and version comparisons for the same song, the individual song names are not announced in the audio recordings. Each tune should be recognizable, and the track numbers are easy to reference with the specific versions in the book—beside the titles, as well as in the Table of Contents.

PREFACE

This book contains arrangements for all levels of players to enjoy. It also includes arrangements for the player who is ready to move to the next level. If an arrangement seems too simple, look behind it—there will be another version and alternate licks. These are derived from arrangements that I have used with my students and in my own performances. Each can be learned as written, or the alternate licks can be used in place of the corresponding measures to form an entirely different version. The measures are numbered so that you can insert these into the correct measures. Each song includes musical notation and tablature, as many mandolin players prefer to have both options available.

The Ultimate Mandolin Songbook is a challenging title and one I have endeavored to justify. The publisher named the book, and together we determined which song titles were to be included. All of the songs are well-known and respected in a particular musical genre, great mandolin tunes, and special in some way—either in the history of music, through its composers, and/or in bluegrass music in particular.

A brief history is included with each song. Many of the lyrics are also included. I hope this will enhance the player's appreciation for each song as well as his/her understanding of the song and its roots. Interestingly, during my research, I discovered that several of these songs are official state songs. The research stemmed primarily from encyclopedias, magazine articles, internet, original scores, and album liner notes.

With the word "ultimate" in mind, I tried to include songs from a variety of musical styles: bluegrass, ragtime, swing, pop, rock 'n' roll, and jazz. These are arranged in a variety of picking styles: tremolo style, double stops and harmony notes, traditional bluegrass styles, the melodic/fiddle style (i.e., "Roanoke"), jazz and ragtime patterns, triplet style (i.e., "How Great Thou Art"), crosspicking (i.e., "You Are My Sunshine"), and a combination of these. These will be identified when they are applied. The first version for each song is a traditional arrangement that establishes the melody. Each subsequent version will build upon this, in varying degrees of complexity.

The arrangements are written in the key for which the song is traditionally played. There are songs in minor keys and modal keys as well as major keys. When there are vocals, an alternate version may be included in a different key. Chord symbols are also included, along with explanations when these help to understand the song.

The songs include a wide variety of tempos, from slow to breakdown speed. Also, waltzes are contrasted with the standard 4/4 time, and ragtime, bluegrass, swing, and jazz rhythms can be found.

Each song can be played for enjoyment alone by learning the version of your choice, or, for the more ambitious, a study on improvisation with multiple versions is offered with each song. There are infinite ways to arrange one song for the mandolin. Alternate licks are included with each version to a) simplify, b) make more difficult, c) embellish, d) offer a different effect, e) offer a different picking style for a tune, and more.

These arrangements have been very effective with my students, and I hope you will enjoy them also. As always, happy pickin'!

Janet Davis

INTRODUCTION & GUIDELINES

ALTERNATE LICKS

Alternate licks are included after almost every song. These are interchangeable measures that can be substituted in the actual arrangements. Each lick is numbered so that it corresponds with the same measure number(s) in the arrangement. Although each arrangement can be enjoyed as it is written, these licks can be used for a variety of purposes. If an area of an arrangement is too difficult, look for an alternate lick for that measure. For the more advanced player, if you want to embellish the arrangement or make it more intricate, look for an alternate for that purpose. These licks can also be used to create an entirely new version. Also, look for recurring patterns. The following are interchangeable D chord licks (as found in "Foggy Mountain Breakdown"):

NOTE: Occasionally, the same lick may be played for two entirely different chords. This happens when the notes in the lick belong to both chords.

PICK-UP NOTES

Each arrangement begins with a measure labeled "pick-up notes." These are notes that lead into each arrangement. Two or more arrangements or versions for the same song can also be combined with one another through the pick-up notes. To link two arrangements, the measure labeled "pick-up notes" at the beginning of the second arrangement should be played in place of the *last measure* of the first arrangement (e.g., measure 32). In other words, substitute the pick-up notes of the newest version for the last or final measure of the previous version. These notes connect the music smoothly between two versions.

NOTE: If a rest occurs at the beginning of the pick-up notes, you can substitute the first note of the measure being replaced, then continue with the pick-up notes (see example 2 below).

MEASURE NUMBERS

The measures in each arrangement are numbered above each measure. You can follow the measure numbers like a trail, from start to finish, which will also help with the repeated sections. The measure numbers are also intended to help you interchange ideas from version to version. It may also help to understand that traditional music usually works with multiples of four-measure phrases—4, 8, 16, 32, etc. Like sentences, musical phrases usually consist of four measures each. It is also fun to substitute whole phrases from one version to another.

SECTIONS—FORM

When learning a new song, it is usually best to learn it one section at a time. Sections will be indicated in the arrangements—i.e., sections A and B for fiddle tunes; Verse and Chorus for songs with lyrics; or others: sections A, B, C, D, etc.

NOTE: A typical Verse (or Chorus) for a song will contain sixteen measures (a total of four phrases of four measures each). Notice that often the first eight measures sound like a question, and the next eight measures sound like an answer. Traditionally, the Verse and Chorus together will total 32 measures.

TABLATURE & RHYTHM

All arrangements are presented in standard notation and tablature for the mandolin. Standard tablature indications for hammer-ons, pull-offs, and rhythmic indications, etc., are used throughout this book. (A brief explanation of how to read tablature is also included at the end of this section for those who are new to tab.) The following should also be noted:

NOTATION:

Tuning: The mandolin is tuned exactly like the fiddle: G(4th string)–D(3rd)–A(2nd)–E(1st).

= **Implied note or "ghost" note:** A note in parentheses is optional but should be accounted for in the timing. (Sustain the previous note through this beat if you omit this note.)

= **Implied or optional chord:** A chord in parentheses may be substituted for the standard chord indicated.

= **Double Stop:** Two notes played simultaneously—a two-note or partial chord.

= **Tie:** Two identical notes are "tied" together. Only the first note is played. Sustain or hold this tone through the second note; i.e., do not pick the second note.

= **Slur:** Two different notes are connected. The second note is usually sounded by a left-hand technique (slide, pull-off, etc.).

⌒ = **Fermata:** This symbol over a note means to sustain it longer than the stem indicates.

> = **Accent:** Emphasize the note—i.e., play it louder.

· = **Staccato:** Do not sustain if this appears over the note; it should be short and sharp.

≋ = **Tremolo:** Right-hand picking technique that involves rapidly picking the string(s) with the flatpick in a continuous back-and-forth motion. This is often used on the mandolin when a note is held over several beats. Tremolo can also be used for an entire song, especially when the emphasis is on the melody notes. (See next page for more explanation, under "Rhythm").

⊓ = **Downstroke:** Pick down toward the floor.

∨ = **Upstroke:** Pick up toward the ceiling.

‖: :‖ = **Repeat Sign:** Play again before continuing. Return to the previous repeat sign if there is one; otherwise, return to the beginning and repeat the section. The measure numbers also indicate the repeats.

|1.   ‖2.   = **Endings 1 and 2:** Play through Ending 1 to the repeat sign, then repeat the section, substituting Ending 2 the second time.

D.S. al Coda: Return to the sign (usually Section A) and repeat until "To Coda." Then skip to the Coda (Ending). Used at the end of a song, this usually indicates a section is to be repeated before the Ending (Coda).

LEFT-HAND TECHNIQUES:

Harm. --| = **Harmonics:** This can be seen in "Orange Blossom Special." When this dashed line appears over a section of the music, the notes should be played as chimes or harmonics. Very lightly place a left-hand finger across the strings directly over the metal fret bar at the indicated fret. Pick the indicated string with the right hand to play the chimes. Do not depress the string to the fingerboard. This will only work over certain fret numbers (i.e., 5th, 7th, 12th, 19th, etc.).

h = **Hammer-on:** Pick a string and sound a higher note with a left-hand finger *without picking* it. This note is sounded only by the left hand.

s = **Slide:** Pick a fretted string and move to a different note with the same finger still depressed *without picking the second note.*

NOTE: A slide may also be sounded between two picked notes.

p = **Pull-off:** Sound the note with a left-hand finger by pulling off the string. Pick the string for the previous note, then pull off the string with the left finger to sound the note indicated with the pull off. *Do not pick the second note* with the right hand.

RHYTHM:

Rest: This indicates silence. Do not play for the equivalent number of beats indicated by the rest.

𝄽 = **Triplet:** Three notes are played in same amount of time as two eighth notes.

𝄎 = **Tremolo:** This involves continuously and rapidly picking the string down and up with the right hand to sustain the note(s) over the correct number of beats. The tremolo should be continuous and played for the duration of the note. All of the notes in a song may be played this way, so there is no interruption from the pick from note to note, or only the notes that are sustained for longer durations can be played with the tremolo. There are many ways to vary this. The right wrist should be relaxed, so that the picking hand is tremulous. This is a beautiful way to play a melody on the mandolin. (Children learn this easily if you tell them to pretend they are very old and shaky.)

HOW TO READ TABLATURE FOR THE MANDOLIN

The *four lines* represent the *four strings* of the mandolin. (NOTE: Each line equals two strings on the mandolin.)

The top line is the E or 1st string (highest pitch) ⟶

The bottom line is the G or 4th string (lowest pitch) ⟶

NOTE: If you lay your mandolin in your lap, the strings will match the tablature.

The *numbers* on the lines represent each fret number, which you will hold down on the string (line) before picking the note. (A "**0**" means to play the string "open" without fretting it.)

Bar lines will be placed in your songs to separate the beats into measures. Generally, there will be 8 eighth notes or 4 quarter notes per measure. You should accent the first note of each measure.

The *pick direction* will alternate: down–up–down–up in order to play the music smoothly.

IMPORTANT:

Rhythm for the tablature is reflected by the corresponding notes in the musical notation above the tablature.

Left-hand fingerings for the tablature are indicated (suggested) with numbers beside the *noteheads* in areas of the song which may be difficult to play.

Key of C

ALABAMA JUBILEE

Words by Jack Yellen   **Music by George Cobb**

"Alabama Jubilee" is a popular ragtime tune composed in 1915. It has been recorded on many instruments in a variety of musical fields. In the bluegrass world, it is usually performed as an instrumental (without the vocal part). A favorite among mandolin players, the following arrangements for this tune are played in the key of C. Notice that the chord progression works along the circle of fifths. It begins with the A chord and travels from V–I chords until it finally lands on the C chord, which is home base.

You ought to see Deacon Jones
Rattle them old bones
Old parson Brown, he's dancin' round like a clown
Old Aunt Jemima, past about eighty-three
Shoutin' I'm full o' pep
Watch your step! Watch your step
Uncle Joe danced aroun' on his toe
Picked them up and hollered, let 'er go
Oh, honey, hail! Hail! The gang's all here
For the Alabama Jubilee

Version 1: Melody

The following arrangement is based upon the basic melody for this tune. Feel free to add tremolo to all or any areas, or play it exactly as written. This is a basic variation upon which the following arrangements will be built. For embellishment, the open-string notes may be doubled by playing the same tone on the lower, adjacent string at the seventh fret. (See the A chord alternate licks for an example.) Although not required, you may find it easier and smoother when you add tremolo. Left-hand fingerings are indicated in numbers next to the noteheads.

NOTE: To repeat this version, follow measure 32 with measure one of another version, or substitute its last three beats with the pick-up notes. Also sustain the dotted half note through three beats: ♩. = ♩♩♩ (3 beats).

TRACK 1

Key of C

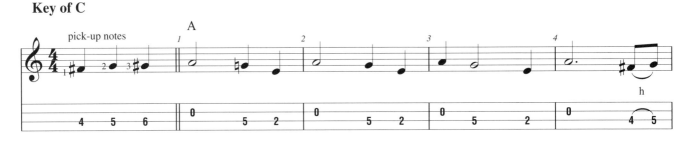

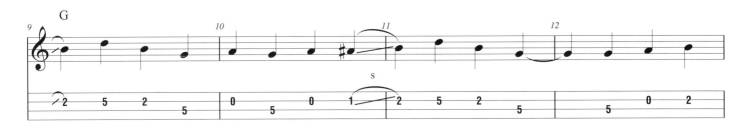

Alternate Licks

The following licks can be used for Version 1 by substituting the lick for the corresponding measure number(s). Notice how the overall flavor of the song can change just by using a few different licks.

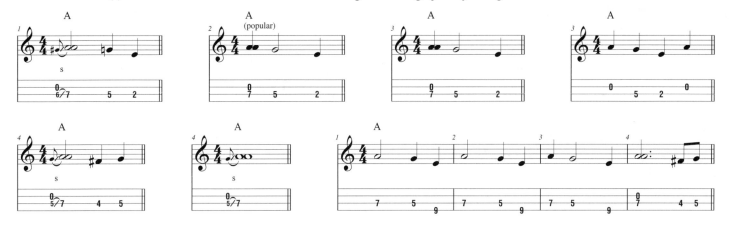

Version 1: Alternate Licks (cont.)

Version 2: Embellishing the Melody

You can add embellishment to the melody with eighth notes (or tremolo), double stops, or lick substitution. Doubling the open A string by playing the 7th fret D string is optional. See alternate licks to simplify measures 1–4.

TRACK 2

Version 2: Embellishing the Melody (cont.)

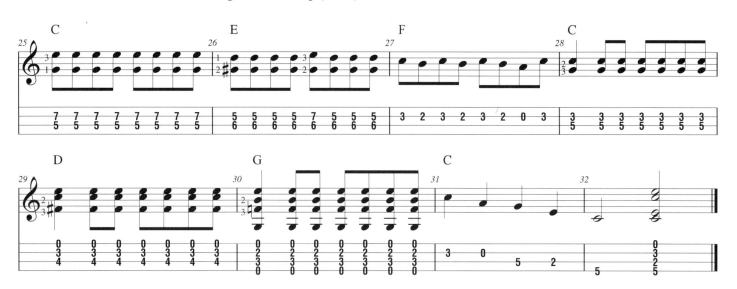

Alternate Licks

The following licks can be substituted for Version 2's corresponding measure numbers. Some of these licks will be more effective if they are substituted as a group. Experiment and have fun interchanging these. These may also be used for Version 1.

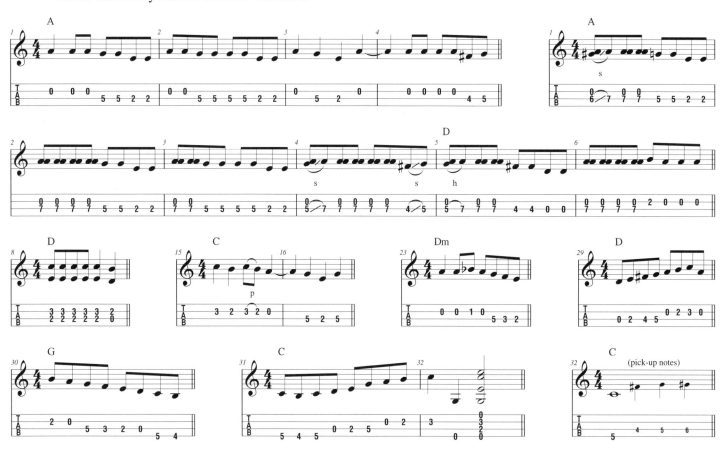

Version 3: Adding Chords and Licks

This version can be a lot of fun to play, beginning with a rhythmic A7 chord. Notice how much this small change creates an entirely new variation. This is followed by a scale-based lick (A Mixolydian) that lands on the A note. The D chord emulates what is played for the A chord in the beginning four measures. The G chord licks are based on the *G Mixolydian mode* (C scale starting on G). Keep in mind that measures 1–8 can be used in any version. Substitute the first set of alternate licks for measures 1–2 and notice that you have instantly created another version.

TRACK 3

15

Alabama Jubilee

Version 3: Adding Chords and Licks *(cont.)*

Alternate Licks

16

Version 4: Alternate Lick Substitutions

This version builds on Version 3 by substituting several of the alternate licks. The purpose is to demonstrate how easy it is to create a new variation. The main changes are in measures 1–2 for the A chord and measures 5–6 for the D chord. Notice that this sounds entirely different from Version 3 with just these small changes. Also, for fun, the C chord fill-in licks for measures 13–16 and the G chord's measures 9–11 change only one note. The scales beginning in measure 29 add drive to the end of the song in a strong, bluegrass fashion.

TRACK 4

Version 4: Alternate Lick Substitutions (cont.)

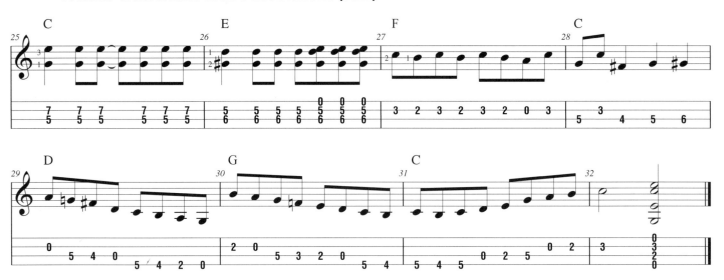

Alternate Licks

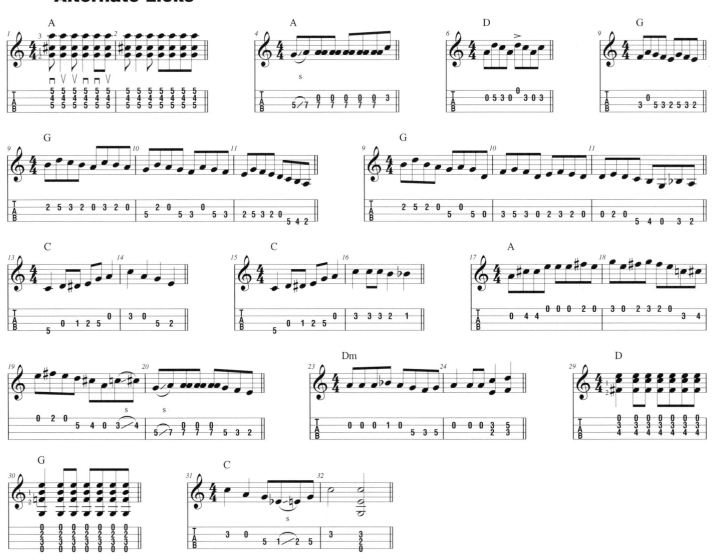

Version 5: Building with Licks

Notice that this starts out like Version 4, but the D and G chord licks have changed. Practice these patterns by themselves and learn to use them according to the chord indicated. Add them to your vocabulary of licks, and improvising will soon become increasingly easy and natural.

TRACK 5

Version 5: Building with Licks (cont.)

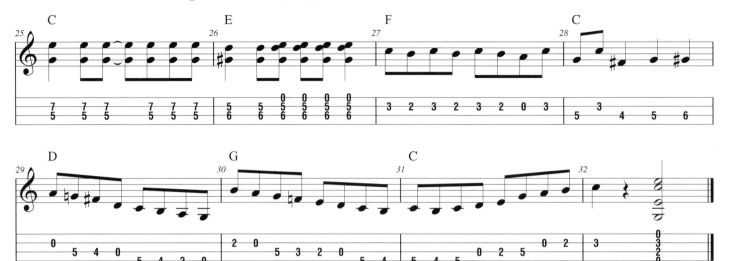

Alternate Licks

Additionally, the alternate licks from the previous versions will also work for Version 5.

Version 6: Bluegrass Style

The syncopation used in measures 1–8 is based on an often-used Bill Monroe pattern. Instead of changing notes on the expected beats, each new note occurs on the upbeat, adding bluegrass energy and drive. This version builds on Version 5 by retaining the patterns of measures 5–8 and 17–20. See the alternate licks for a fun way to end this version.

TRACK 6

Key of C

Alternate Licks

Version 6: Alternate Licks (cont.)

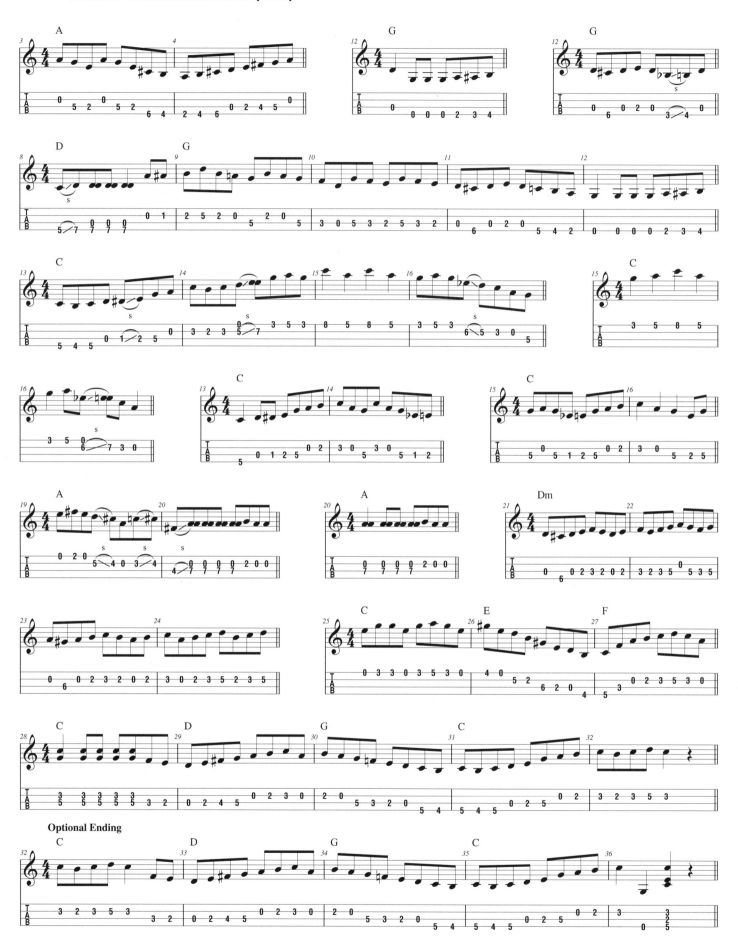

Version 7: Jazzing It Up

For the Advanced Player

Notice that the opening measures are based on the main motif of Version 6. However, the tones in this pattern belong to an A9 chord (A–C♯–E–G–B). This retains the Monroe-style syncopated pattern, but changes the notes for a more colorful jazz-like sound. Notice the alterations of otherwise standard licks using extended chords, chromaticism, altered scales, and left-hand techniques (slides, hammer-ons, pull-offs, etc.).

In measure 8, the eighth notes are included to make it easier to play in time. For a more jazz-like effect, play only the first note of the phrase.

TRACK 7

23

Version 7: Jazzing It Up *(cont.)*

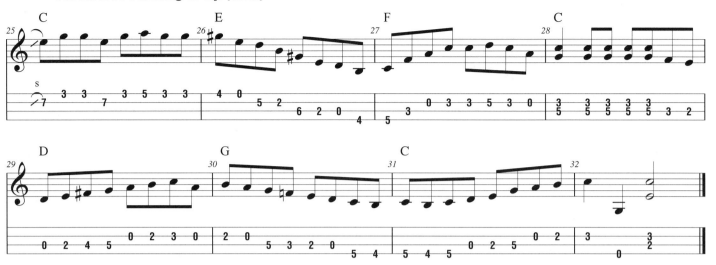

Alternate Licks

The licks that are several measures long may be broken up and used individually as well.

AUTUMN LEAVES

English Lyric by Johnny Mercer   French Lyric by Jacques Prévert   Music by Joseph Kosma

"Autumn Leaves" has, through the years, become one of the most popular songs of all time in both French and English languages. It has been recorded by many top artists in pop as well as in the jazz world, where it is often performed as an instrumental tune. The tune is natural for the mandolin, and the chords offer harmonies that will thrill any audience.

This song was originally written in 1945 as a French tune—"Les Feuilles Mortes," which, literally translated, means "Dead Leaves." The music was composed by Joseph Kosma, and the original lyrics were written by poet Jacques Prévert. It was introduced in the film *Les Portes de la Nuit* in 1946. Fortunately, for the English speaking world, American songwriter/performer, Johnny Mercer, wrote English lyrics for this beautiful tune in 1947. In 1955, this tune hit #1 on the American charts with Roger Williams' (pianist) rendition selling over a million copies. In 1956, the film *Autumn Leaves*, starring Joan Crawford, featured this song, sung by Nat King Cole, as the title track. From that point forward, "Autumn Leaves" has been considered a popular classic, recognized and performed by people of all ages. Audiences love to hear it, and musicians love to play it.

> *The falling leaves drift by the window*
> *The autumn leaves of red and gold*
> *I see your lips, the summer kisses*
> *The sun-burned hands I used to hold*
>
> *Since you went away the days grow long*
> *And soon I'll hear old winter's song*
> *But I miss you most of all my darling*
> *When autumn leaves start to fall*

Version 1: Melody

To learn this version, it may help at first to play without using tremolo. This will help you hear the melody with the correct timing. Tremolo can be added for every note throughout the entire arrangement or only for the longer note values. This melody is beautiful and should be played with expression; in other words, play this as you feel it. Slides are indicated as options in several places, which add embellishment to the effect. Optional harmony notes are included in section B, and when more than one note is indicated, the main melody note is the highest note.

TRACK 8

Key of E minor

Version 1: Melody *(cont.)*

Alternate Licks

Version 2: Embellishing the Melody

Apply tremolo and slide into notes as you develop your own version. This version builds on the melody and works just as well at slow or faster tempos. Section A2 (measures 17–32) is a fun and optional variation to repeating section A1. Once you make your choice (use your ears), move on to section B to conclude this beautiful piece.

TRACK 9

Key of E minor

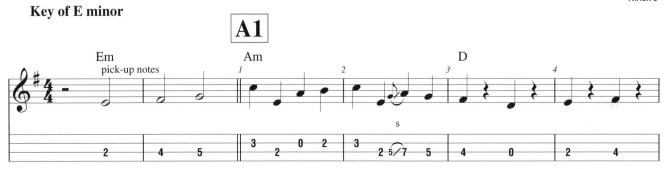

Version 2: Embellishing the Melody (cont.)

Alternate Licks

Version 3: Adding a Touch of Swing

This version adds harmony notes, triplets, grace notes, and rhythmic syncopations. Slides, pull-offs, and hammer-ons are suggested for left-hand articulations. Also, extensions for the back-up chords are offered in order to lend a more jazz-like feel to the accompaniment.

NOTE: Play through this without the full chords or left-hand techniques until you are comfortable with the version. Also, although measure 1 starts on an Am7 chord, it serves as the iv chord for the actual key of E minor.

TRACK 10

Key of E minor

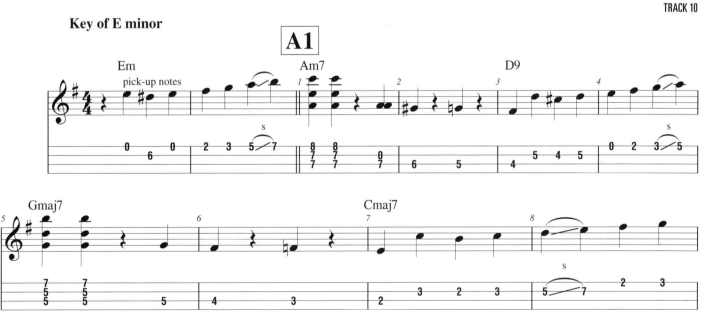

Version 3: Adding a Touch of Swing *(cont.)*

Alternate Licks

Version 4: Bluegrass Style

The following is a bluegrass variation on Section A. It should be played up-tempo in a melodic/fiddle style. To combine this Section A with Section B of any other version, play measure 31 from the desired version, instead of measure 32, and continue on to that version's Section B. It is very effective to play Version 4 after another version is played slowly (i.e., play Version 1 slowly, then transition to an up-tempo Version 4).

NOTE: Section A is played twice, so follow the parenthetical measure numbers the second time through. This requires you to jump to the second ending after the B chord measure.

TRACK 11

Key of E minor

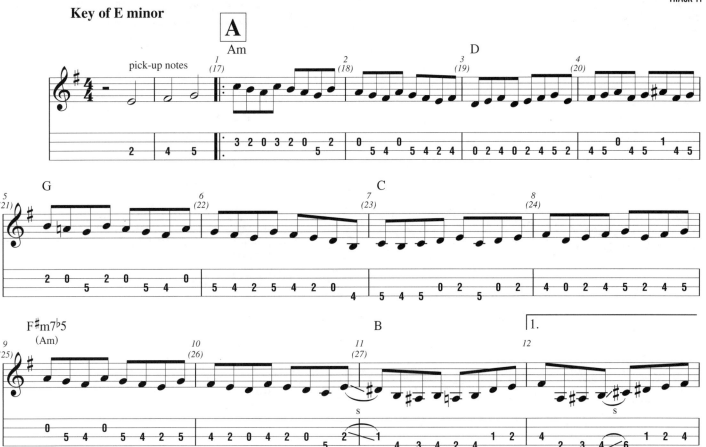

Version 4: Bluegrass Style (cont.)

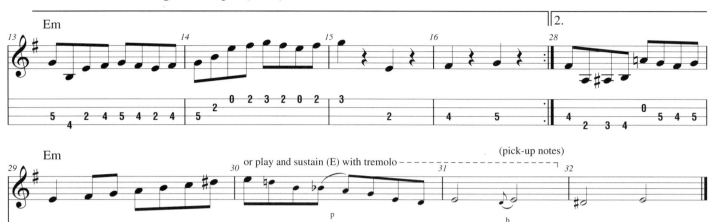

Alternate Licks

Pick-up notes to measure 17 for alternate Section A2.

Alternate Licks: Up-the-Neck

This can be used entirely for Section A, or for measures 17–32, creating a nice contrast when repeating the form. Follow measure 32 with Section B from any version.

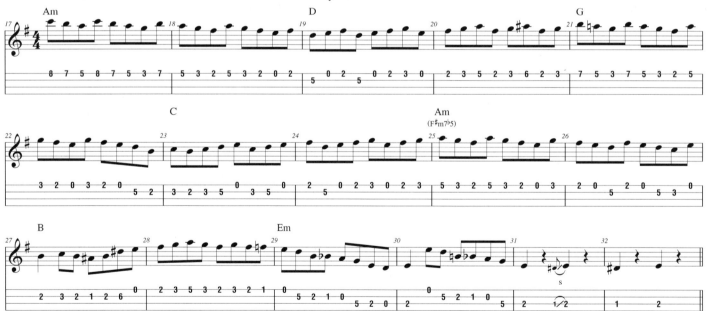

To play Section A entirely up-the-neck, play the above measures twice, but substitute the following measures the first time through (for measures 28–32).

DEAR OLD DIXIE

By Lester Flatt and Earl Scruggs

Today, "Dear Old Dixie" is among the most popular bluegrass instrumentals of all time, and has been recorded by many great artists. This tune is especially fun to play on the mandolin. The melody is tuneful and energetic with a chord progression so full of motion that any picking style on the mandolin is effective. In fact, Earl Scruggs chose to play "Dear Old Dixie" for Bill Monroe as one of two instrumental tunes when he first joined Bill Monroe's Bluegrass Boys in 1945. He felt it had a uniqueness that was an excellent contrast to "Sally Goodin'" (the other tune he chose to play). It is interesting that both songs are played in the higher register of the instrument, yet they sound completely different. The idea for the song was based on a performance by Snuffy Jenkins. When Flatt and Scruggs formed their own band in 1948, the Foggy Mountain Boys, "Dear Old Dixie" began to shine, especially as a banjo and fiddle tune. When they recorded it for Columbia, in 1952, the banjo and fiddle took turns trading leads. As more and more musicians heard this tune, more and more instrumentalists learned it. Today, "Dear Old Dixie" is not only a bluegrass standard, but also an ultimate mandolin song from start to finish. It is fun to play for all levels. Among the many professional mandolin players who have recorded this tune are Sam Bush, David Grisman, Roland White, Ricky Skaggs, Bobby Osborne, and Bobby Clark.

The melody for "Dear Old Dixie" has a certain familiarity about it that may remind one of the well-known "Dixie," written by Daniel Emmett in 1859, which became the anthem of the southern states in the Civil War.

The chords used in this song also lend to its success. The chord progression begins with the standard I–IV (G–C) in the key of G. The tension begins to build when *secondary dominants* (temporary "V chords" of other diatonic chords) are introduced; for example, the A chord in measures 13–14 is a V of V (D). Here the band stops playing for a brief Dixie-style solo announcement from the lead instrument. The second half begins like the first half, but suddenly goes to the B chord: V of vi (Em). Now, cleverly, instead of going directly to the expected Em chord (as many tunes do by following the circle of fifths), the B moves to C (IV), then to G (I), and finally to E *major*, which acts as a V of ii (Am). The E moves to A major (another secondary dominant), which continues around the circle of fifths with the D (V) and G (I) that follow. The energy and ingenuity of the chord progression adds a driving force and excitement to end the song for a smiling audience.

Version 1: Tremolo-Style Melody

The melody is very effective when played tremolo style. Notice that the first of each eighth-note group is the main melody. Play them as written or tremolo the notes as fast as you can feather the strings (usually resulting in triplets). To help you emphasize the melody, the bare-bones melody format is offered directly after this version. When playing through this, notice measures 17–22 are identical to measures 1–6. Seeing patterns like these cut down on your repertoire study time.

The pick-up notes compose a very important motif of this tune. Its restatement in measure 8 is noteworthy as well. Measures 15–16 are signature lines to this song, letting you go, "Hey, this is 'Dear Old Dixie.'" The band usually *tacets* (stops playing) for these measures to emphasize this passage.

NOTE: The last three notes of measure 32 are the pick-up notes to the next version.

TRACK 12

Key of G

Dear Old Dixie

Version 1: Tremolo-Style Melody *(cont.)*

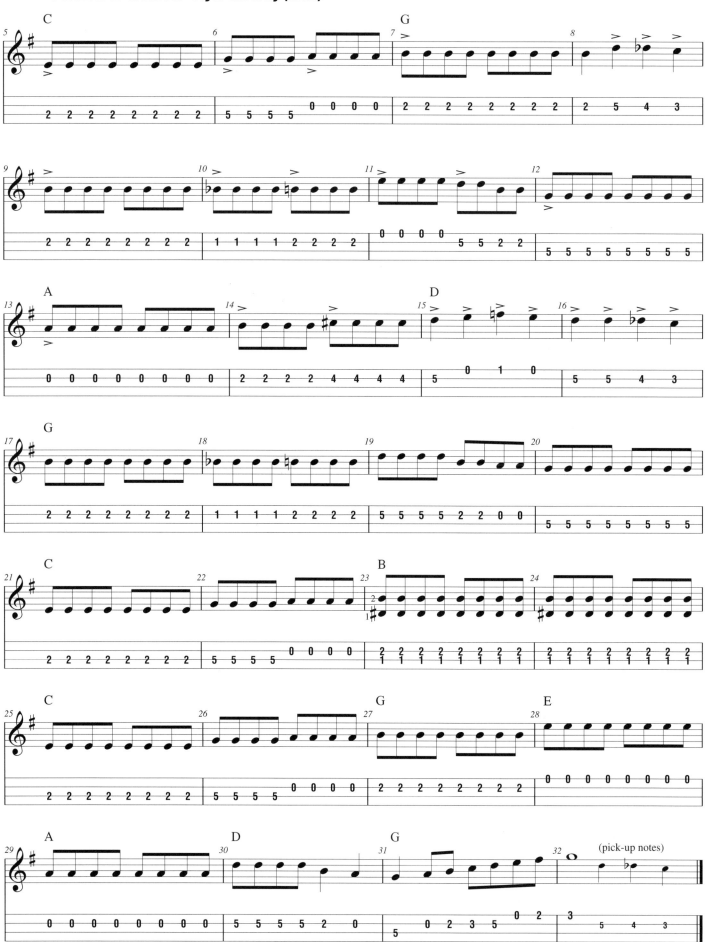

Alternate Version 1: Tremolo-Style Melody

This is Version 1 with tremolo indicated for each single melody note (the notes are the same).

Alternate Licks (both versions)

Version 2: Adding Bluegrass Licks and Double Stops

This begins with harmony notes as double stops, but the left-hand fingering is not as difficult as it sounds or appears. The bluegrass licks start at measure 5. Study their harmonic context and get in the habit of applying them to as many other songs as you can for the same chord(s). For example, measures 5–6 contain licks for a C chord, so you can go back to "Alabama Jubilee" and try that same lick there.

TRACK 13

Key of G

Alternate Licks

Keep in mind that measures from other versions of the same song can be applied to the above arrangement.

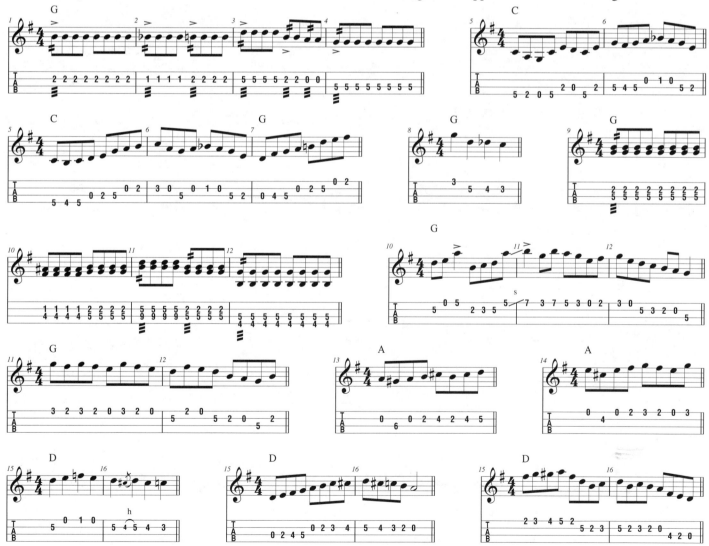

Version 2: Alternate Licks (cont.)

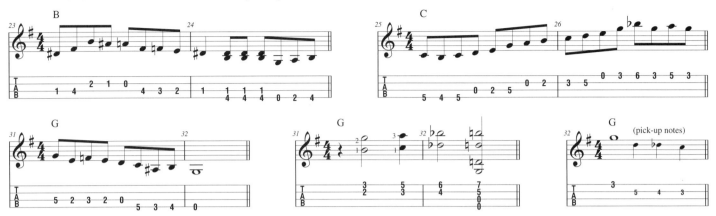

Version 3: Substituting Licks by Chord

This bluegrass arrangement is based on Version 2; notice the substitutions for measures 1–4, 9–13, and 17–20. By changing licks that establish the melody, it is very simple to create a new version. Try identifying the other areas that have changed and notice the applicable chord(s). To further develop this arrangement, use the corresponding alternate licks for measures 5–8. While changing ideas is all well and good, the arrangement as written is fun to play also.

TRACK 14

Key of G

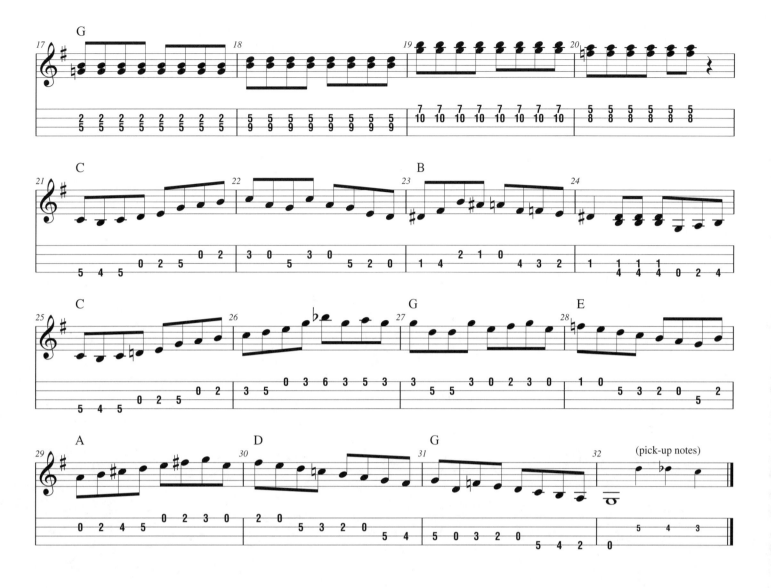

Alternate Licks

Substituting the following measures into the above arrangement, no matter how few, drastically changes the effect of the music, creating a new version. Learn the patterns below as two-measure phrases for the appropriate chord, and you could apply them to as many songs as you like.

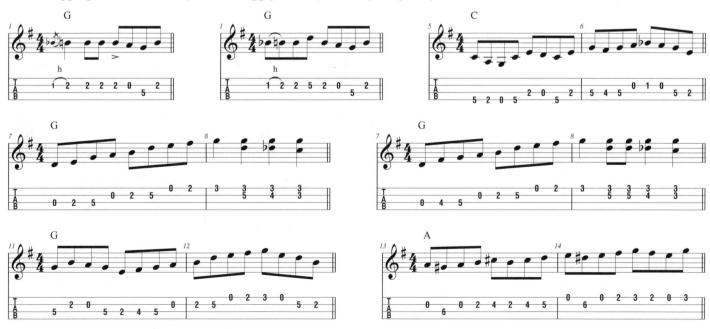

Version 3: Alternate Licks (cont.)

Version 4: Building a New Arrangement

This bluegrass arrangement is included primarily to take the "lick substitution" concept one step further. Based on Version 3, it substitutes alternate licks for several of the inside chords in an effort to demonstrate how easily a new version can be derived. The following arrangement uses new patterns for measures 5–6 over the C chord and 7–8 over the G chord. Because the D chord in measures 15–16 is so essential to the overall effect, this has also been changed. Notice how measures 21–22 and measures 5–6 are identical.

TRACK 15

Version 4: Building a New Arrangement (cont.)

Alternate Licks

For more ideas, return to previous versions of "Dear Old Dixie" and draw from the arrangements as well as the alternate licks of each version. Similarly, the licks for measures 30–31 will substitute nicely for measure 29–30 of "Alabama Jubilee" (the function of the D and G chords in both songs are the same).

Optional Ending

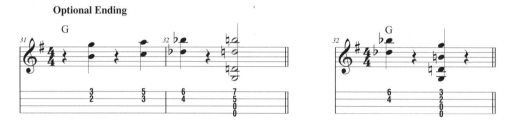

EAST TENNESSEE BLUES

Folk Song

Although titled a "blues," this tune might be more appropriately described as a "rag." The syncopated timing and the happy-go-lucky feel make this popular tune fun to play and a crowd pleaser. The origin of "East Tennessee Blues" can be easily traced back as far as the 1920s, when Charley Bowman, a champion fiddler from East Tennessee, recorded it for Brunswick Records. Fiddlin' Charlie Bowman, also popularly called "Tenn-O-See Charlie," won contests all over Tennessee as well as in nearby states. The Bowman Brothers made numerous recordings and played in New York, Washington D.C., and along the East coast as well. Their music became extremely popular, even among politicians, for whom they performed at numerous political events. They performed and recorded so often that "East Tennessee Blues" had plenty of exposure. People often attribute this tune to Charlie as his own composition, which it may well have been.

The form, melody, chords, and rhythms in "East Tennessee Blues" could almost be considered a prototype for country-style ragtime music. As with many tunes that are passed down through the generations, new artists have adapted it to their own style and for their own instrument. Bobby Hicks, a popular bluegrass fiddler, has made "East Tennessee Blues" part of his repertoire for many years and has often been credited with popularizing this song, especially among bluegrass and country musicians. Numerous mandolin players have recorded this tune, and some have developed their own compositions that seem to be based upon these ideas. Jethro Burns' "Kelly Boy Rag," a mandolin tune that appeared on several of his albums, resembles this tune. Jack Tottle wrote a wonderful tune for the mandolin titled "East Tennessee Rag," which he recorded with Béla Fleck. A third part is added on his arrangement where the chords work along the circle of fifths. Although the original version for "East Tennessee Blues" has two parts, musicians today often include a third part as well.

As you play through this, notice that the opening motif, which is played for the C chord in the first phrase, is also played for the F chord in the second phrase. The left hand uses the same pattern on the fingerboard for both chords; it just moves over one string. This is one of the reasons this tune is so much fun to play on the mandolin. The fingerboard patterns tickle the fingers, and the syncopated ragtime rhythms tickle the ears. It is a natural tune for the mandolin.

Version 1: Ragtime on the Mandolin

In this arrangement, look for the repetition of licks for each chord, as this will make the song easier to learn. Section B is actually a variation on Section A where only certain measures have been altered. In Section A, measure 6, the tied note through beat 3 is a staple of ragtime rhythm and is exhibited throughout. Section C is optional and has been recently added to the repertoire of bluegrassers; it's also a blast to play. Beginning on the A chord, it works through the circle of fifths with secondary dominant chords to land back on C.

TRACK 16

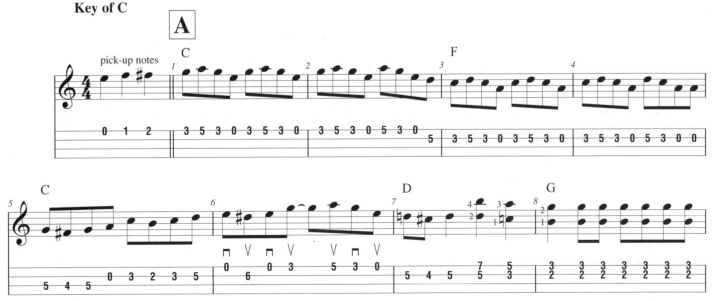

Version 1: Ragtime on the Mandolin (cont.)

Section C (Optional)

This section may be added as a third part. The original 1920s version only contained Sections A and B.
There are two alternate licks for measure 48 that serve as a turnaround with pick-up notes to the A section.

Alternate Licks

Where do you start—at the beginning, or just by substituting any random measure? Either way, each lick will slightly change the effect. Let's get to it.

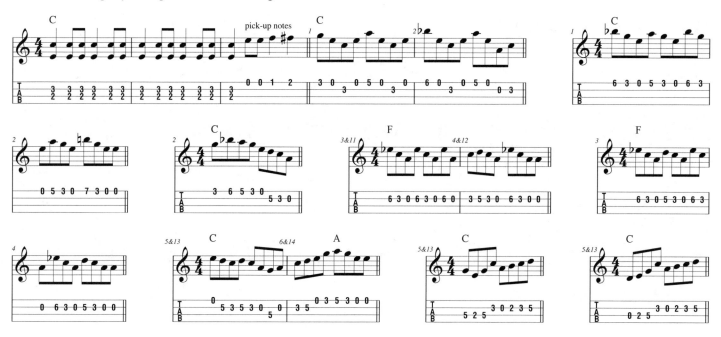

Version 1: Alternate Licks (cont.)

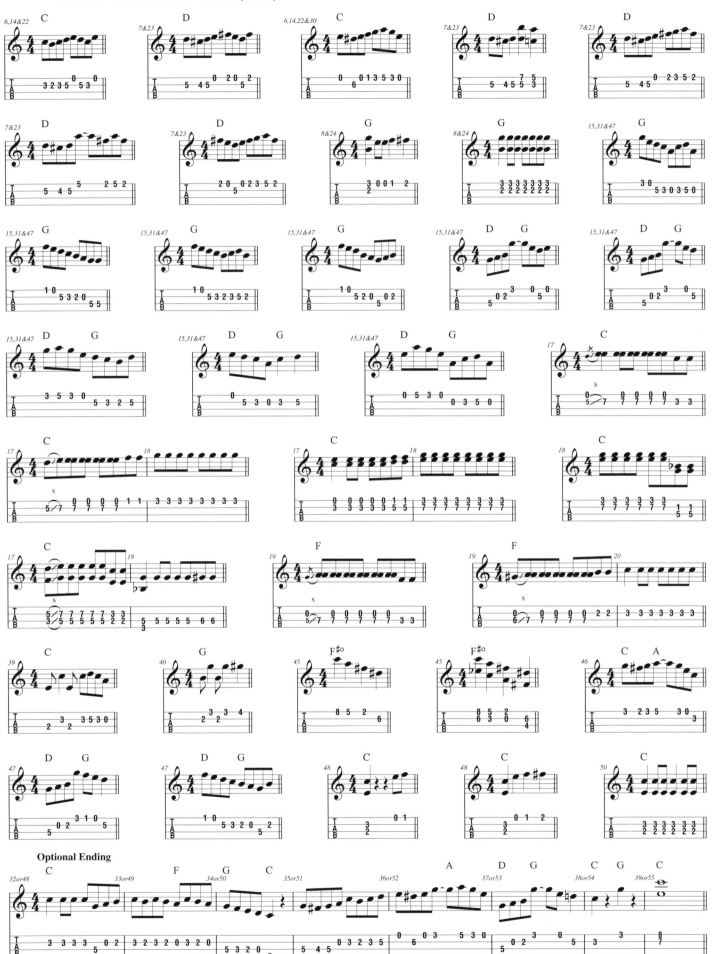

Version 2: Jazzing It Up

Section A starts differently from Version 1 to give it the effect of a second variation. Version 2 uses an alternate pattern for measures 15, 31, and 47, changing only two notes for a different flavor. Also, for these measures, the back-up can either use a D–G, G, or Dm–G chord sequence. Section E harmonizes the melody of Version 1. It also uses the same chord sequence as Section A. Technically, this could be considered Section A2, but the melody is a signature of this song's B section. There are a lot of substitution choices, so feel free to alter it as you wish.

TRACK 17

Version 2: Jazzing It Up (cont.)

Alternate Licks

Many alternate licks for Version 1 will also work for Version 2.

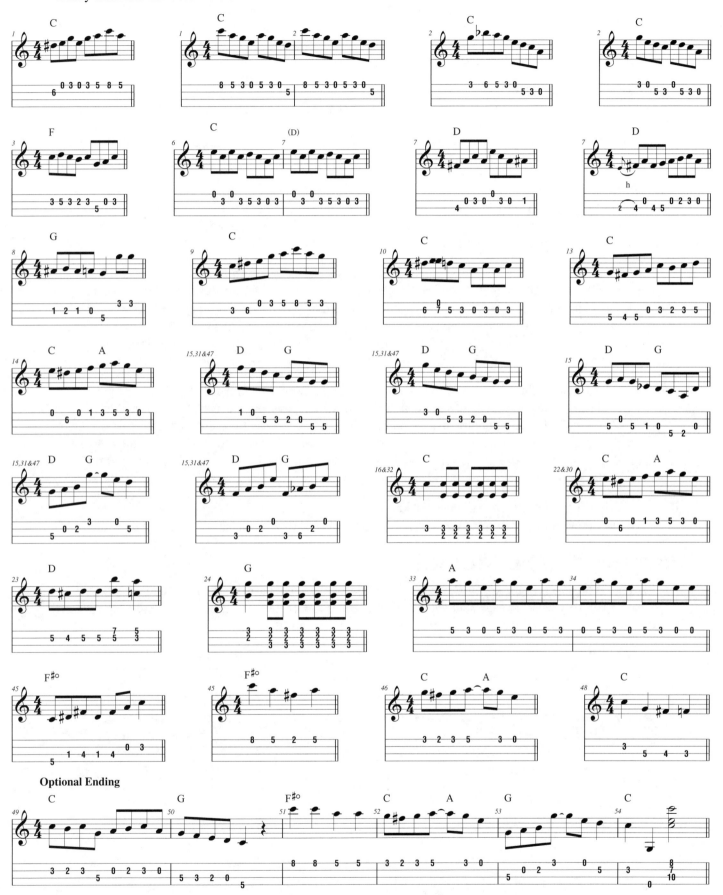

Optional Ending

EIGHTH OF JANUARY

Traditional

This traditional fiddle tune is well-loved and recognizable to people of all ages. It was written to celebrate the U.S. victory over the British in New Orleans on January 8, 1815, and to honor Andrew Jackson for this victory. Originally titled "Jackson's Victory," this song was often performed as a fiddle tune at square dances and other festivities that celebrated the anniversary of this battle—especially in the South.

This was the last major battle of the War of 1812, where the intent of the British was to take over New Orleans and the surrounding areas. Although a treaty had already been signed in December to end the war, this news did not reach the troops in New Orleans in time to prevent the battle. Jackson's popularity grew as well as the fiddle tune honoring him. As a result, Andrew Jackson eventually became the seventh president of the United States in 1828.

During the Civil War, Andrew Jackson's political views fell out of favor, and the name for the song was changed to "Eighth of January." Migrant workers who left the dust bowl of Oklahoma and moved to California also helped popularize this tune in the Western part of the United States. Lyrics have also been written through the years, including a version written by Mary Sullivan Shafter in 1940.

In the mid-twentieth century, "Eighth of January" reached its highest recognition and achievement since its origin in 1815. In 1958, Jimmy Driftwood (James Morris) wrote lyrics for this tune, which he titled and recorded as "The Battle of New Orleans." As a school teacher, he wrote numerous songs to entertain and educate his students about historical events. This tune became an instant hit. Johnny Horton's recording of "The Battle of New Orleans" went straight to #1 on the charts in 1959. That year, this song won a Grammy for Song of the Year, and Johnny Horton won the Grammy Award for Best Country and Western Performance.

Since 1815, "Eighth of January" has been and continues in the twenty-first century to be recorded by countless bluegrass and country bands, remaining a favorite at festivals and events. Often played in the key of D, especially on the mandolin and the fiddle, this tune is also easy to transpose to other keys. Banjo players prefer the key of G, but it's easy for a mandolin player to transpose it to G, D, or A simply by playing the same fingerboard positions starting on the string named for the key (i.e., use the D string if the song is in the key of D).

The following arrangements are written in the key of D using D, G, and A chords. Each note can also be moved up or down an equal distance on the same strings to change the key alphabetically along the scale line.

Version 1: The Melody

This song is arranged in the key of D, using the D major scale as the basis for the notes and chords. Version 1 is a very basic arrangement with a few challenges (alternate picking, string-skipping, etc.). Look for patterns and notice how many times a note or idea is repeated.

TRACK 18

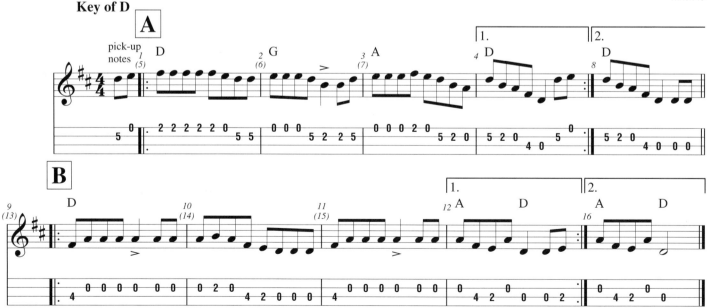

Version 2: Fiddle Style

This builds on the previous version by emulating a fiddle with more scale-like runs and syncopated rhythms (see measures 9 and 11). The form has both sections played twice, but replaces each eighth measure with a transitional measure that leads more smoothly to the next section.

TRACK 19

Optional Introduction

This four-measure phrase is a decisive intro to be played before measure 1. Notice that beat 4 of measure 4 is the same as the pick-up notes to the original introduction.

Alternate Licks

Version 3: Adding Chromaticism and New Melodic Notes

Originally, these measures were to be included as alternate licks for Version 2. However, they work so well together, I've combined them as an additional variation. This version adds chromatic notes for interest, color, direction, and energy. Section A's chord progression is the simple I–IV–V (D–G–A), while Section B uses only the I–V chords, (D–A).

NOTE: Each measure of the following arrangement can be superimposed into Versions 1 and 2 for their corresponding measure numbers, and vice versa.

TRACK 20

Alternate Licks

Version 4: Adding Left-Hand Techniques and Blues Notes

Watch out for the triplet figure in measure 4. Pick the first note, hammer-on, then pull-off all in one beat. For fun, plug Section B into any of the other versions. Notice the bluesy ideas with the use of ♭3rds and ♭7ths. Compare Version 4 to Version 3 and notice how it builds on the techniques discussed.

TRACK 21

Key of D

Alternate Licks

Measures 17–20 make up an optional ending to any version you'd like.

Version 5: Up-the-Neck and Crosspicking

This version is a fun one. Concerning pick directions, there are different opinions about picking across three strings, but most people use the crosspicking technique developed by Jesse McReynolds. This follows a banjo-style roll with down–up–up picking starting with the bass string. Notice that the open strings are allowed to ring—that's the beauty of crosspicking. (Alternating the pick direction is also effective, especially when consecutive notes are on one string.)

NOTE: The left-hand hammer-ons and slides in measures 9–12 are optional. Also, see "You Are My Sunshine" for another crosspicking arrangement.

TRACK 22

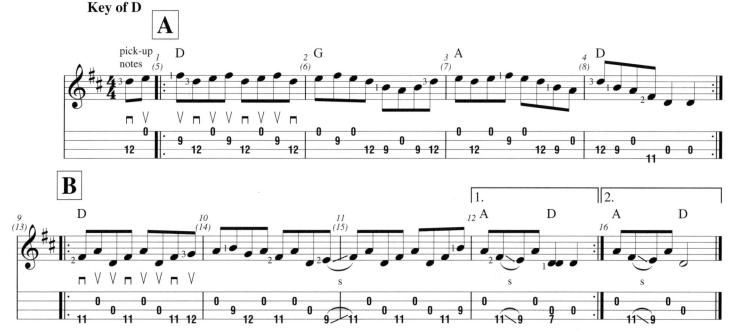

Alternate Licks

Alternate Version 5

This is offered to help you easily hear the main melody notes. The use of alternate picking is most effective for this lower-melody arrangement. The notes are the same as in Version 4, played in the open string area.

Key of D

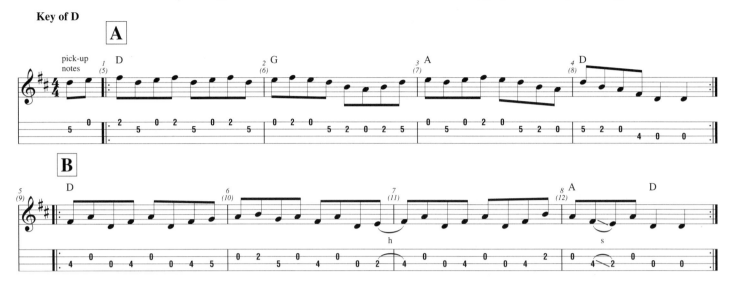

EL CUMBANCHERO

Words and Music by Rafael Hernandez

This delightful rumba has been recorded by numerous artists from a variety of musical genres, including rock, salsa, rap, reggae, bluegrass, jazz, and just about any type of music imaginable. It is usually performed as an instrumental and has been performed on many different instruments as well. This tune has also become a standard among marching bands at football games across the nation. And "El Cumbanchero" is an exceptional mandolin tune! Jesse McReynolds (of Jim and Jesse fame) has greatly contributed to its popularity as a mandolin instrumental. David Grisman also has an excellent recording of this tune, as do many other mandolin players and bluegrass musicians.

Rafael Hernandez was born in Puerto Rico, where he studied music on a variety of instruments. He has been credited with composing over 3000 songs and is well-known for his dance tunes, romantic boleros, and patriotic tunes. Hernandez served in the U.S. Army during World War I as a medic in France where he wrote "Oui Madame." In 1929, Rafael became the first Puerto Rican composer to sign with Peer International, one of the largest U.S. publishers. It has been reported that Rafael was not especially fond of "El Cumbanchero," but it nevertheless became so well-known that President Kennedy addressed him as "Mr. Cumbanchero."

The following arrangements are in the key of D minor, but the B section is in D *major*. Version 1 is very much like the original composition and should be fun for every level of player. Version 2 expands upon this and is a true bluegrass version, full of drive and suspense.

The introduction can be played at a dramatically slow tempo, or it can be played up-tempo, setting the stage and pace for the tension and excitement about to take place. It can also serve as a very effective ending.

Section A starts with a bang at a very lively tempo and with a melody line that primarily emphasizes the root (D). However, this section closes with an exciting run spiraling down the D minor scale—this is where the audience really comes alive and where musicians can really shine in their interpretations.

Section B changes the mode from minor to major. The melody works with the chord tones in this section. Beginning in the key of D major, it moves through the key of E and finally lands on a pivot chord (A) to return the song to D minor. The A pivot chord is common to both keys. It is the IV chord in the key of E and the V chord in the key of D minor.

NOTE: "El Cumbanchero" is derived from the *son* (a rumba played in double time).

Version 1: Melody in D Minor

This tune begins with a dramatic introductory section played at a slow tempo, but measure 9 begins with the song's usual up-tempo pace—though the tempo change is at the performer's discretion. While the Intro and Section A are in the key of D minor, Section B provides a nice contrast by modulating to D major. However, the IV chord is G *minor* (iv) to retain the flavor of the D minor key. To conclude the form, Section A is played again. **Form: Intro–Ⓐ–Ⓐ–Ⓑ–Ⓐ–Intro to end**

TRACK 23
(Played w/o repeats)

Key of D minor

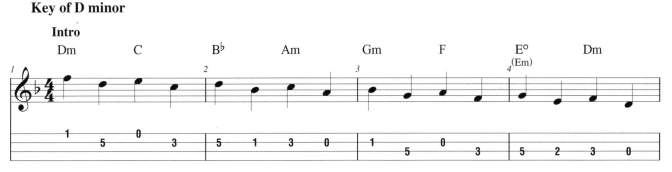

El Cumbanchero

Version 1: Melody in D Minor (cont.)

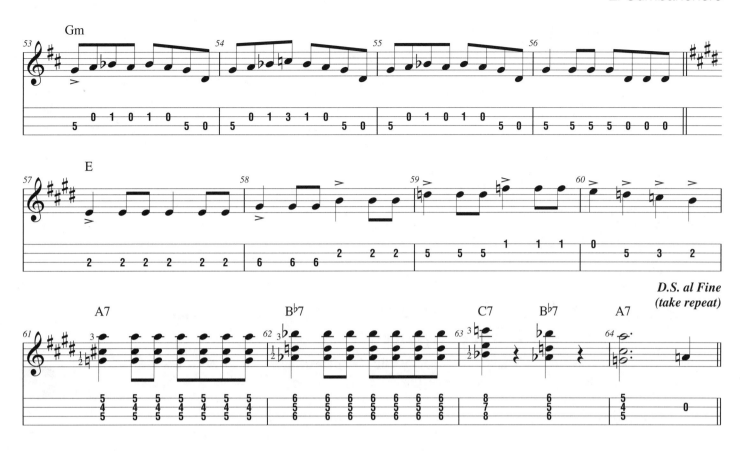

D.S. al Fine
(take repeat)

Alternate Licks

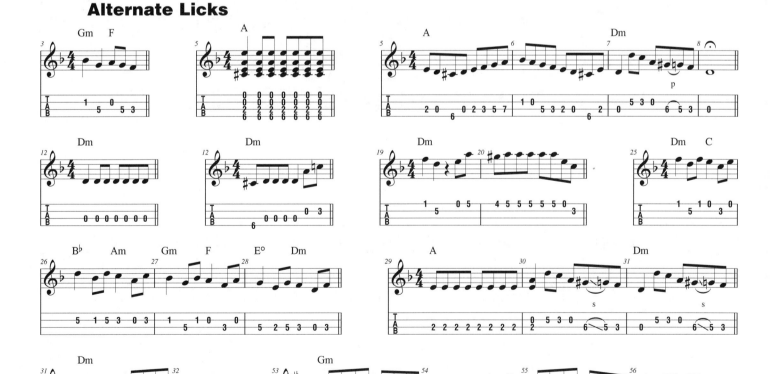

Version 1: Alternate Licks *(cont.)*

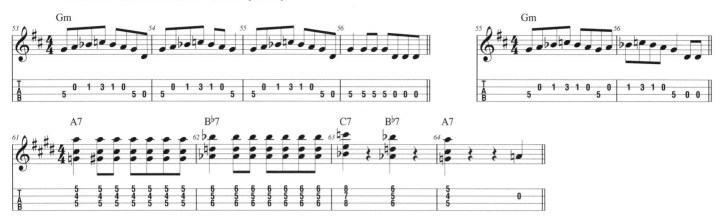

Version 2: Embellishing with Slides, Runs, and Syncopation

There are many fun and different ways the descending D minor scale in Section A (measures 25–32) can be played to excite an audience. Play a straight tremolo as written in Version 1, use the circular scale (below), or see the alternate licks for more ideas.

TRACK 24
(Played w/o repeats or Coda)

Key of D minor

Intro

Version 2: Embellishing with Slides, Runs, and Syncopation (cont.)

Alternate Licks

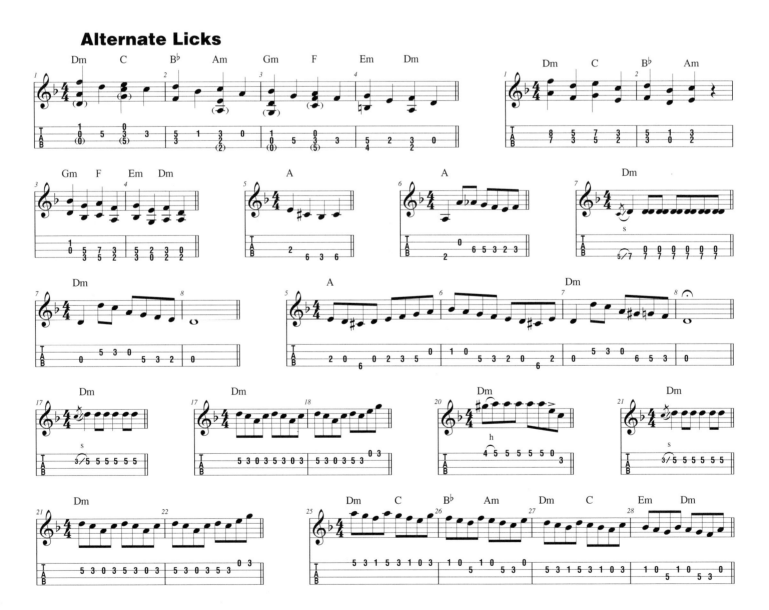

Version 2: Alternate Licks (cont.)

THE ENTERTAINER

By Scott Joplin

Many people agree that Scott Joplin is today recognized as one of the most important and influential ragtime composers of all time. Born in Texas in 1868, he was the son of a former slave who had been freed only five years before Scott's birth. His mother raised five children as a laundress, singer, and banjo player. From a musical family, he also had some formal music training as a child. At fourteen, after his mother's death, Scott left home and supported himself as a traveling musician along the Mississippi River. However, his dream was to gain recognition as a respected composer. In 1893, he led a band at the World's Columbian Exhibition in Chicago and managed to publish a few songs. He attended George R. Smith College in Sedalia, Missouri in the mid-1890s while teaching and playing piano (and cornet). Scott then moved to St. Louis, Missouri to be closer to publisher John Stark. "Maple Leaf Rag" was published in 1899 with "The Entertainer" soon to follow in 1902.

In St. Louis, he founded the Scott Joplin Opera Company in an attempt to produce operatic works based on the "syncopated style." By 1907, he had moved to New York, where he continued to publish his ragtime music and finished his opera *Treemonisha*. He tragically died in 1917, without knowing of the astounding recognition his music would receive 50 years later.

In the early 1970s, due to the efforts and recordings of pianist and musicologist, Joshua Rifkin, there was a renewed interest in Scott Joplin's ragtime music. In 1972, the movie *The Sting* took the world by surprise with background music featuring Scott Joplin's music. Many people were amazed that it was composed around the turn of the century and were fascinated with the composer's history and music. Scott Joplin, as a composer, finally achieved the recognition and respect he richly deserved, and in 1976, Scott Joplin was finally awarded a Pulitzer Prize.

There are two essential keys to playing a ragtime tune effectively:

1. The tempo should be upbeat, but not too fast.

2. The syncopated rhythms must be played exactly "right." Each note must be played exactly where it occurs within the measure on the designated part of the beat.

Syncopation refers to notes falling on unexpected beats (off beats). This is what gives the ragtime tune its life and character.

The following arrangements are based upon the original piano score. When played on the piano, the right hand plays the syncopated melody while the left hand keeps a steady bass. In order for the mandolin player to play the syncopated rhythms so that they are on the right beats, ghost notes appear in parentheses to help you play with the right timing. You may later decide to omit these notes by replacing them with rests. These arrangements are in the key of C and can be played as mandolin solos or with a complete band. The piece is divided into four sections. It is usually easiest to learn one section at a time. Optional notes are also included to complete a full chord, which is more difficult to play. To shorten the performance, the four parts may be played in succession without the repeats as on the audio.

Version 1: Ragtime Melody

TRACK 25
(A, B, & D sections played w/o repeats)

Key of C

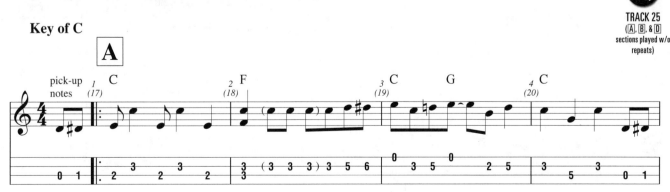

Version 1: Ragtime Melody *(cont.)*

Alternate Licks by Section

Version 2: Adding Harmony and Syncopation

The top note will be the melody note. This is the same as Version 1, with optional harmony notes.

Key of C

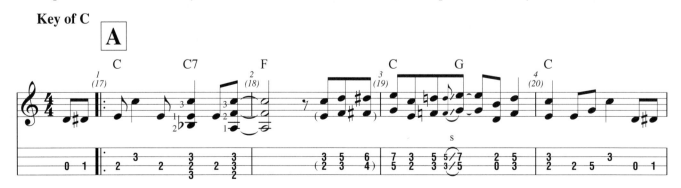

Version 2: Adding Harmony and Syncopation (cont.)

Alternate Licks by Section

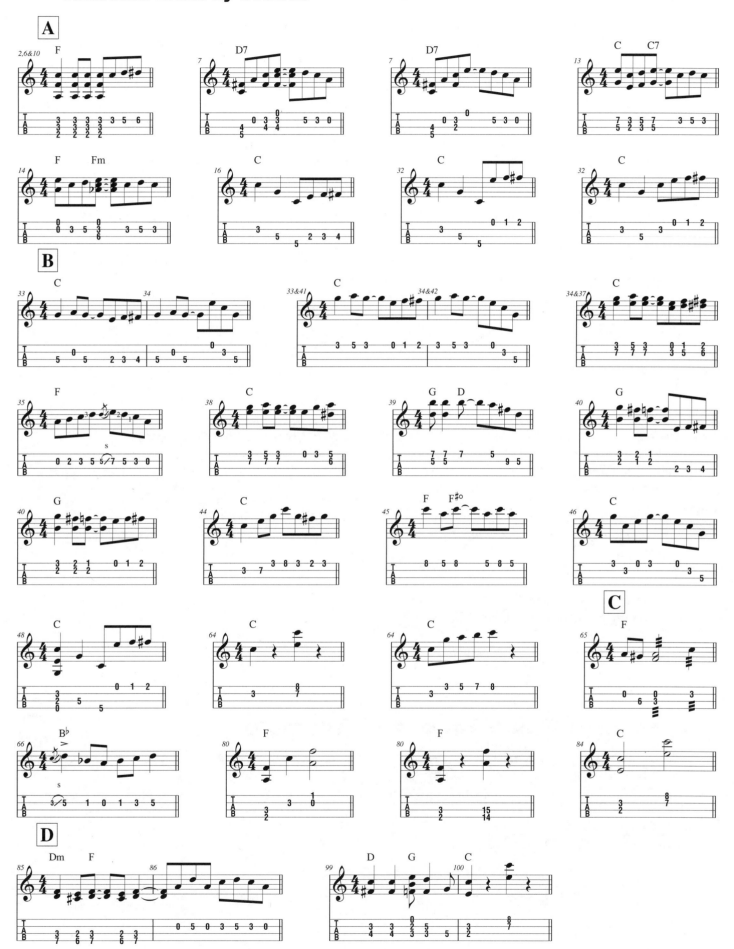

FIREBALL MAIL

Words and Music by Fred Rose

Many professional banjo players learned to play this tune by listening to Earl Scruggs and Lester Flatt on the classic Foggy Mountain Banjo album where it was recorded as an instrumental. The title appeared on Earl Scruggs' original LP as "Fire Ball Mail." With or without the lyrics, this song has become a banjo, Dobro®, mandolin, and bluegrass classic. Mac Wiseman and Roy Acuff have also recorded popular versions with the lyrics.

Four versions are presented here for the mandolin. The first two are standard bluegrass styles—one to be played in the open-string area and one adding harmony notes to standard bluegrass licks. It is a natural style to use the tremolo in this tune due to the long, sustained melody notes. The third version is fun to play once the basic arrangement has established the melody, as it adds blues notes and techniques that give the song a different and entertaining effect. The fourth version is played up-the-neck and returns to the basic tremolo style. However, it also includes licks that drive the music back to the lower tonal area to close the song.

The basic tune for this song uses the G major pentatonic scale tones. The third arrangement adds a modal flavor by including tones from the G minor pentatonic scale.

Here she comes, look at her roll
There she goes, eatin' that coal
Watch her fly huggin' the rails
Let her by, by, by the Fireball Mail

Let her go, look at her steam
Hear her blow, whistle, and scream
Like a hound waggin' his tail
Dallas bound, bound, bound the Fireball Mail

Engineer makin' up time
Tracks are clear, look at her climb
See that freight clearin' the rail
Bet she's late, late, late the Fireball Mail

Watch her swerve, look at her sway
Get that curve out of the way
Watch her fly, look at her sail

Let her by, by, by the Fireball Mail
Let her by, by, by the Fireball Mail
Let her by, by, by the Fireball Mail

Version 1: Basic Tune with Tremolo

TRACK 26

Key of G

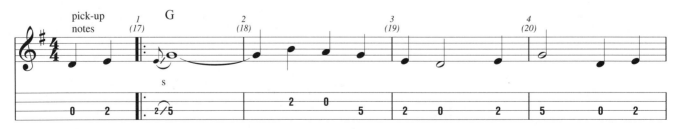

Alternate Version 1

Written in eighth notes, this version might be better to start with—no use of tremolo. After learning the melody with the correct timing, the tremolo should be much easier to add. The melody notes are indicated with an accent.

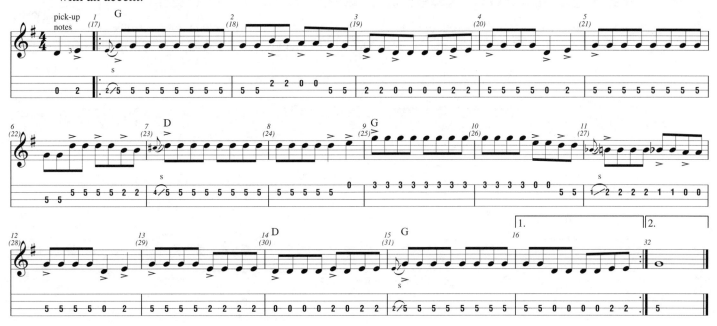

Alternate Licks

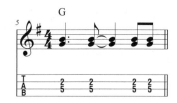

Version 1: Alternate Licks *(cont.)*

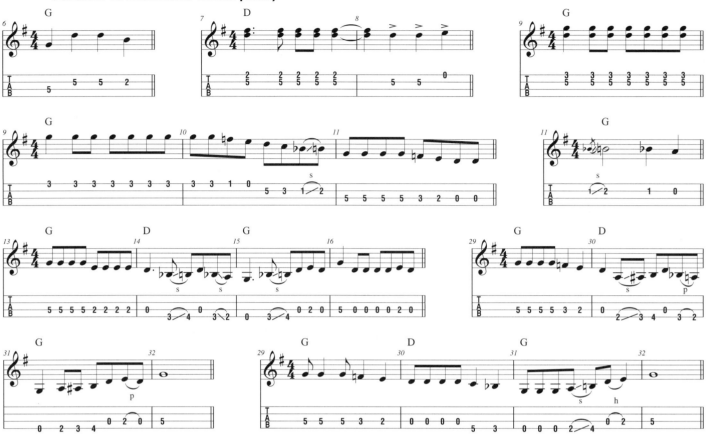

Version 2: Adding Double Stops and Licks

This version opens with a fast slide from the 2nd fret to the 5th on the D string. When *double stops* (two notes played at the same time) are played, the bottom note is the melody, making the harmony note optional.

TRACK 27

Key of G

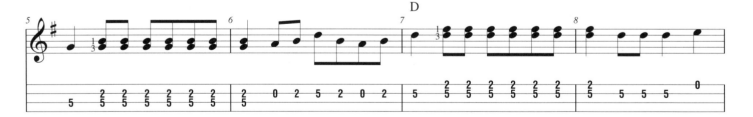

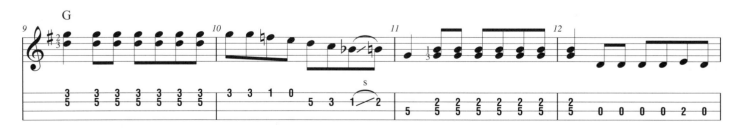

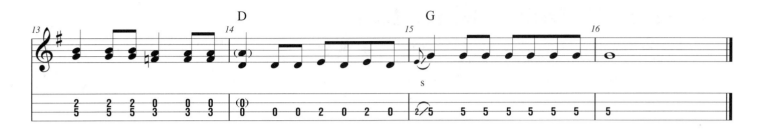

Alternate Licks

Version 3: Adding Blues Notes

This arrangement of the melody uses the G minor pentatonic scale (G–B♭–C–D–F), making for a bluesy sound. To change this to a major-sounding mode, substitute E notes for the F notes. To eliminate the blues effect entirely, change the B♭ notes to B♮. Also, notice the long slides in this version.

TRACK 28

Key of G

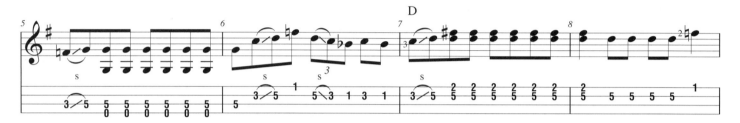

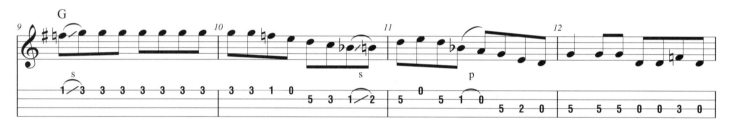

Alternate Licks

Version 4: Up-the-Neck

Here we are going to demonstrate the melody line in the higher areas of the neck. This strategy is useful for the tremolo style, but mixing it up with the alternate licks is a clever artistic move. Instead of playing the music as written, the quarter notes can be converted to eighth notes by playing two notes in place of the one note. This includes the same notes as Version 1, an octave higher.

Key of G

Alternate Licks

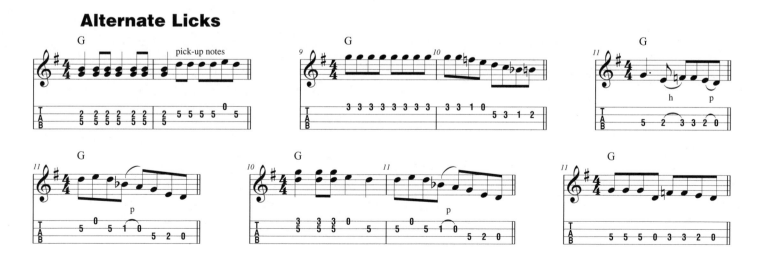

Fireball Mail

Version 4: Alternate Licks (cont.)

FOGGY MOUNTAIN BREAKDOWN

By Earl Scruggs

In 1948, former Bluegrass Boys, Earl Scruggs and Lester Flatt, along with Jim Shumate, Cedric Rainwater, and Mac Wiseman, formed the Foggy Mountain Boys in Hickory, North Carolina. They signed a contract with Mercury Records, and "Foggy Mountain Breakdown" was released the following year. This has continued to be one of the foremost bluegrass tunes of all time. In 1969, the movie *Bonnie & Clyde* used "Foggy Mountain Breakdown" as its theme song, and the world almost immediately gained many new aspiring bluegrass musicians who fell in love with the music, the instruments, this song, and the "new sound." This tune has consistently remained popular in jam sessions as well as in concerts. In 2002, Earl Scruggs & Friends released a new recording for this tune and won a Grammy. Arthur Smith even recorded this tune on the 4-string banjo. The song is perfect for the mandolin, as it can be played in the tremolo style or in the melodic/fiddle style with running scalar lines. It has drive, energy, and a very recognizable melody, which is an achievement for a breakdown.

A "breakdown" is played at a fast and even tempo. The chord progression is a strongly identifiable characteristic in most breakdowns—especially the chord(s) between the I (G) and the V (D) chords. In "Foggy Mountain Breakdown," the E minor chord is the "characteristic" chord in the progression. The original Mercury recording for "Foggy Mountain Breakdown" is interesting because each instrument played the measures for the E minor chord with a different intent. The banjo played each E minor chord for two measures, while the guitar played the E *major* chord for *three* measures, continuing through the measure where the banjo returns to the G chord. The bass, in order to avoid taking sides, plays the E note (the root note of both E major and minor chords). If you try this with other instruments, it may sound funny at first, but this actually creates an appealing dissonance that adds energy to the overall effect—it was certainly successful in establishing "Foggy Mountain Breakdown" as a popular bluegrass tune. Today, the E minor is often played by all instruments for two measures, for the lead and for the back-up; however, some bands will extend the E minor through three measures, while the lead instrument plays the E minor chord for only two measures. To hear this, you might play Version 1 into a recorder and then play the back-up chords along with your recording.

A collection of ultimate songs for the mandolin would not be complete without the inclusion of numerous arrangements for "Foggy Mountain Breakdown." There should be something fun for virtually any level player. For extra fun, an arrangement imitating several of the popular banjo licks, which are easily identifiable in this tune, is also included. Remember, this song can last a long time in a jam session, as it is truly an ultimate bluegrass song.

This song is said to have been based on the Bill Monroe tune, "Bluegrass Breakdown," which Lester and Earl performed while they were with his band from 1945–1948. Using Section A only, the E minor chord was substituted for the F chord to create "Foggy Mountain Breakdown." A few incidental changes were also made, and the B section was omitted completely. Normally, it is played twice in a row with a slight variation the second time.

Version 1: Tremolo Style

Virtually every note in this version should be played with a fast tremolo. Relax your wrist and feather the strings with your pick as fast as you can. Emphasize the first note of each measure to bring out the melody.

TRACK 29

Version 1: Tremolo Style *(cont.)*

Alternate Version 1

Add the tremolo later, after learning the notes and timing.

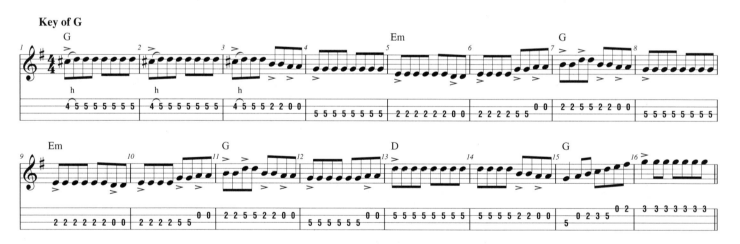

Alternate Licks

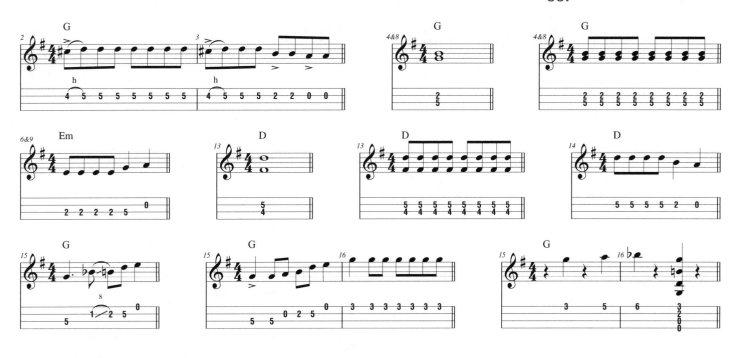

Version 2: Repeat Section

"Foggy Mountain Breakdown" is usually played twice in a row, so this serves as a great repeat for Version 1.

TRACK 30

Key of G

Version 3: Adding Harmony Notes

This arrangement is exactly like Version 2 but with harmony notes. Playing the earlier versions should help keep the melody in your head as these harmonies are added.

TRACK 31

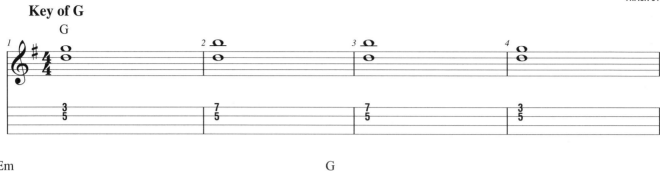

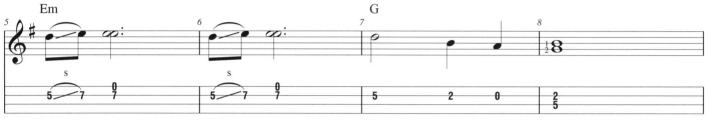

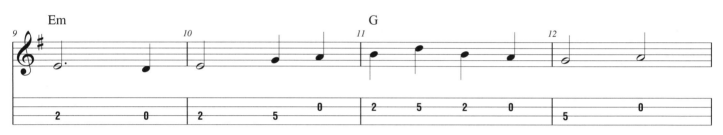

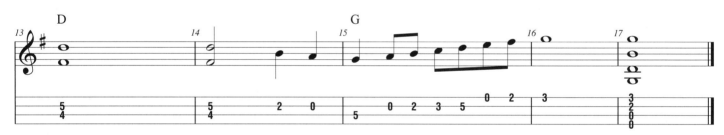

Alternate Licks

Version 4: Adding Bluegrass Licks

In measures 5–7 of this version, the licks work in a circular, scale-like fashion using the G major pentatonic scale. Notice they also add a driving motion to the arrangement without a change in tempo.

TRACK 32

Key of G

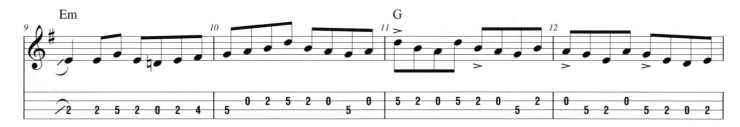

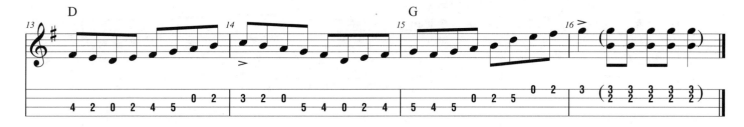

Alternate Licks

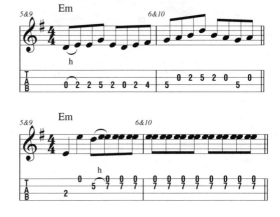

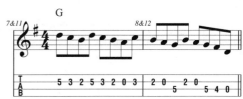

Version 4: Alternate Licks (cont.)

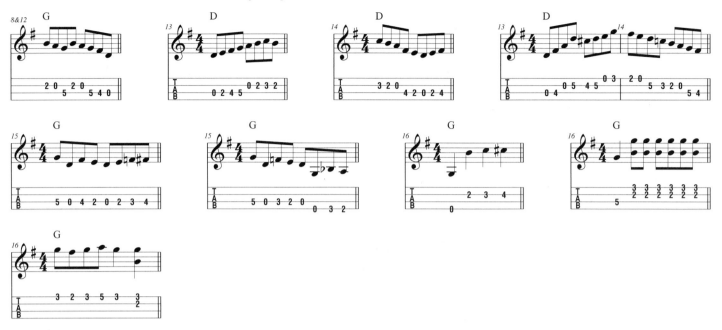

Version 5: Fiddle-Style Bluegrass

This version expands upon the circular scale we discussed in Version 4—typical of fiddle-style bluegrass.

NOTE: Pick-up notes are optional.

TRACK 33

Key of G

Alternate Licks

Version 6: Melodically Banjo-Like

While the opening measures imitate the signature banjo line, measures 9–16 are truly geared towards the melodic style. If you like the banjo ideas, more are offered in the alternate licks section. Interestingly, measures 5–7 can be played again for measures 9–11 and vice versa.

TRACK 34

Key of G

Alternate Licks

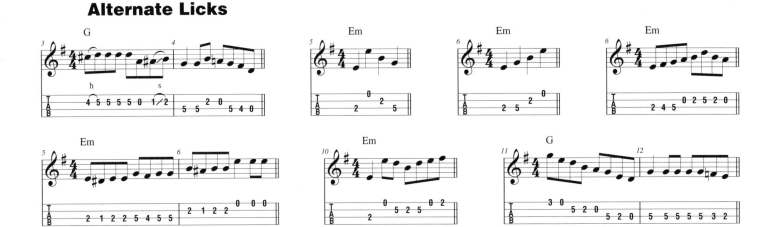

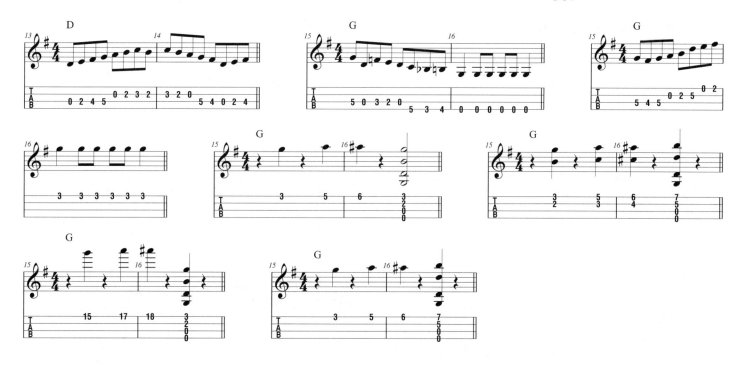

Version 7: Up-the-Neck Licks and Syncopation

This version works well as a repeat section by virtue of these ideas, rather than an opening motif.

TRACK 35

Key of G

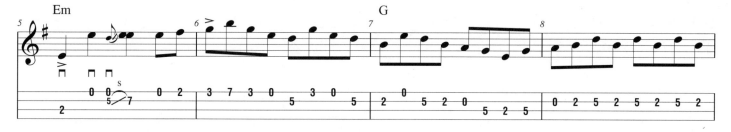

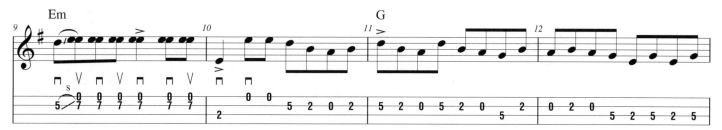

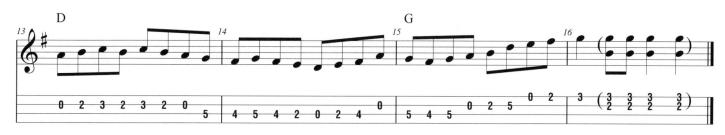

Alternate Licks

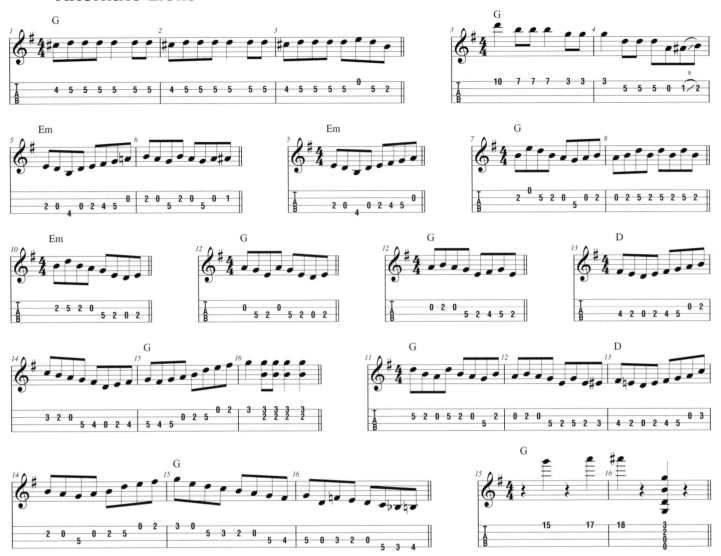

GOLD RUSH
Words and Music by Bill Monroe

Bill Monroe's title as the founder and "Father of Bluegrass Music" dates back to around 1938. During the first half of the twentieth century, the sheer number of popular bluegrass songs he composed and recorded with his band, the Bluegrass Boys, was impressive to say the least. Also of note, many of bluegrass music's top musicians have played with the Bluegrass Boys at some time during their career. In 1970, Bill Monroe was inducted into the Country Music Hall of Fame. In 1986, he was honored by the U.S. Senate as "a force of single importance in our time."

As a mandolin player and admirer of his beloved Uncle Penn who played the fiddle during Bill's childhood, fiddle tunes were among Bill's favorites. Because the mandolin is tuned exactly like the fiddle, these tunes are very adaptable to the mandolin. The "Gold Rush" is a "fiddle tune" written by Bill Monroe, to be performed on the mandolin or the fiddle. This true mandolin tune is very popular at concerts, festivals, and jam sessions and has been widely recorded by bluegrass musicians on a variety of instruments.

This instrumental is normally played in the key of A, based upon the A major scale. Several different versions are presented. The first is an easy-to-play arrangement and is very effective when played live. The third and fourth versions are based on the Monroe style, and the fifth is played fiddle style.

"Gold Rush" is divided into two parts, which is a typical form for most fiddle tunes. It will help to learn Section A first and then work on Section B. Both section A and B are played twice. The first time through Section A, play the first ending; the second time, substitute the second ending: |1. ‖2.

The chord progression for Section A is also common for many mandolin/fiddle tunes. An extended I (A) chord is played through six measures, followed by a quick V (E) in the seventh measure, and a return to the I (A) in the eighth. In Section B, a quick D chord occurs in measures 18 and 22. Back-up musicians usually emphasize this with a quick syncopated brush.

The alternate licks, which appear at the bottom of Version 1, can also be substituted in any other version. Remember to look at the corresponding measure number when playing with these.

Version 1: Bluegrass Style

This should be played at a moderate tempo—not too fast. When combining the versions, play the last measure of the first arrangement as pick-up notes to Version 2, instead of the pick-up notes with Version 2.

Reminder: Play Section A twice, then Play Section B twice.

TRACK 36

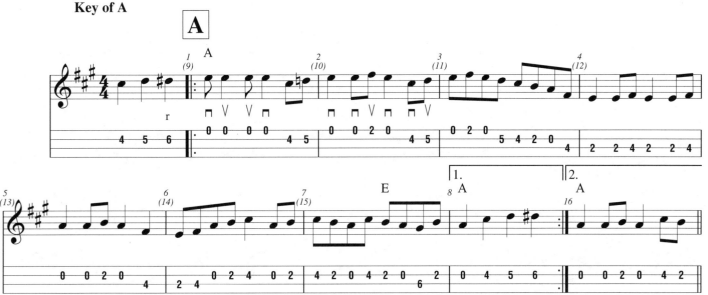

Version 1: Bluegrass Style (cont.)

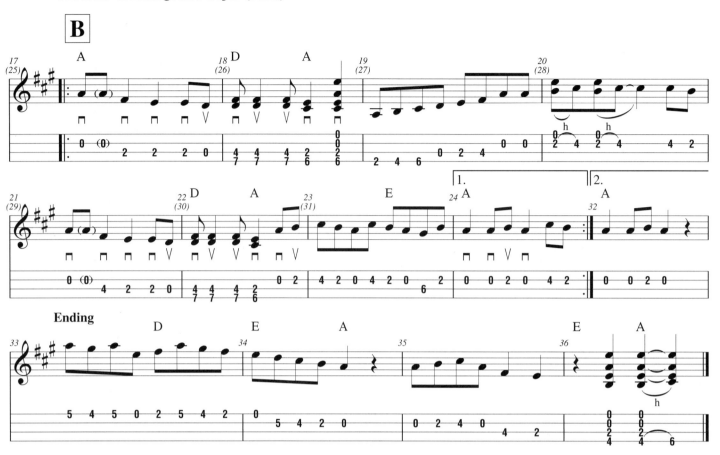

Alternate Licks

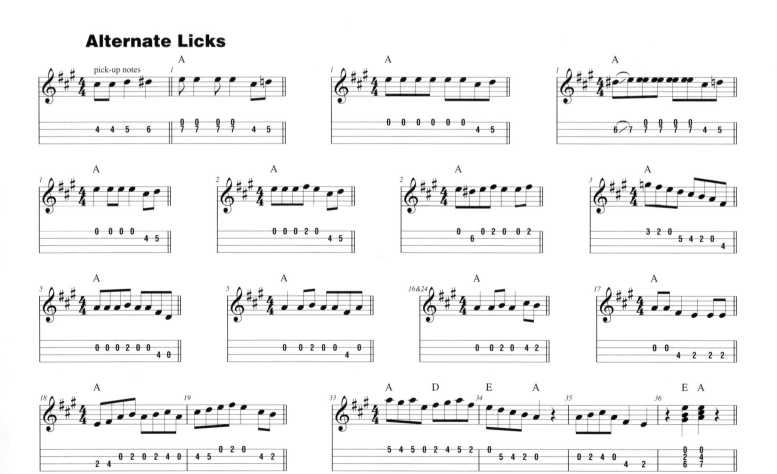

Version 2: Using Connecting Tones

The notes in parentheses are optional. If omitting an optional note, sustain the previous note through that beat.

TRACK 37

Key of A

Alternate Licks

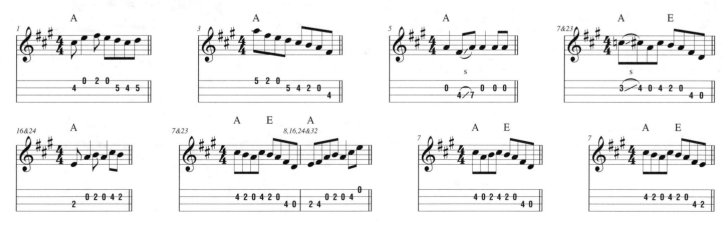

Version 2: Alternate Licks *(cont.)*

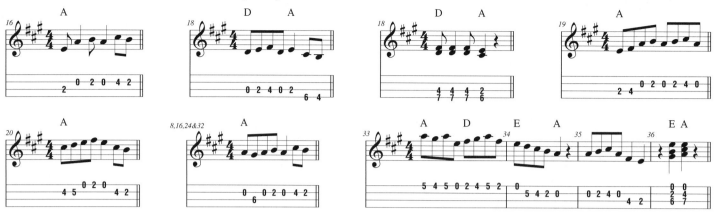

Version 3: Monroe Style

Bill Monroe's mandolin style is characterized with melodic syncopations of the original melody—similar to fiddle shuffle rhythms. Notice how the melody notes change on the off beats ("ands" rather than on beats 1, 2, 3, or 4). Left-hand slides and other staples of his style are omitted for learning ease (see Version 4 for these ideas).

TRACK 38

Key of A

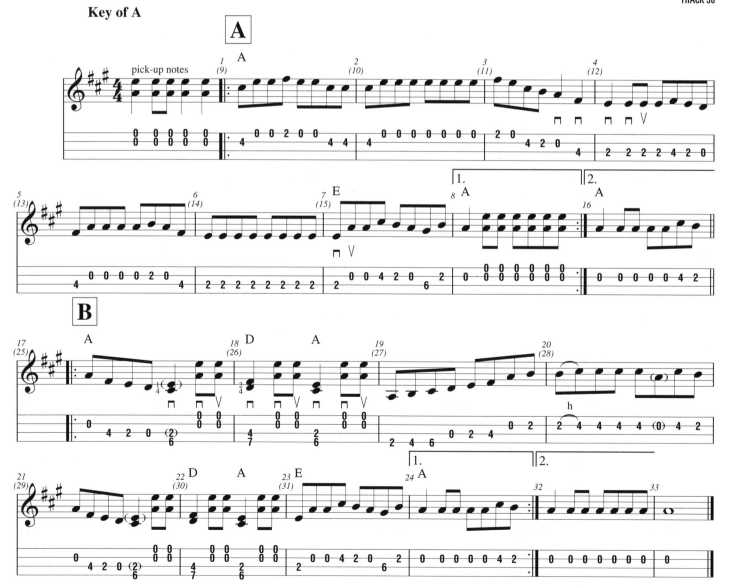

Alternate Licks

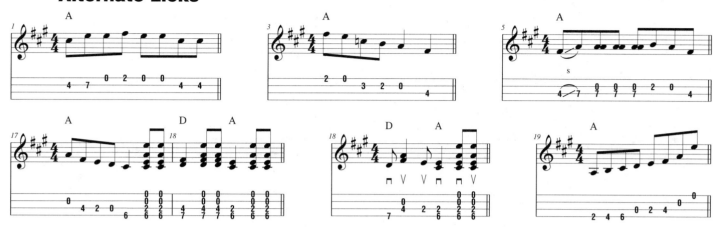

Version 4: Monroe Style with Harmony Notes

Bill Monroe's mandolin style for bluegrass has a very distinctive sound, drawing primarily from fiddle bowing patterns (i.e., see measures 17–18). It often includes open strings as drones to provide harmony with the melody notes. These harmonies and melodies are largely drawn from the pentatonic scales with subtle allusions to the blues scale via the ♭3rd, ♭5th, and ♭7th. Left-hand articulations help emphasize the melody as well.

NOTE: Measures 17 and 18 may be substituted for measures 21 and 22, and vice versa.

TRACK 39

Key of A

Alternate Licks

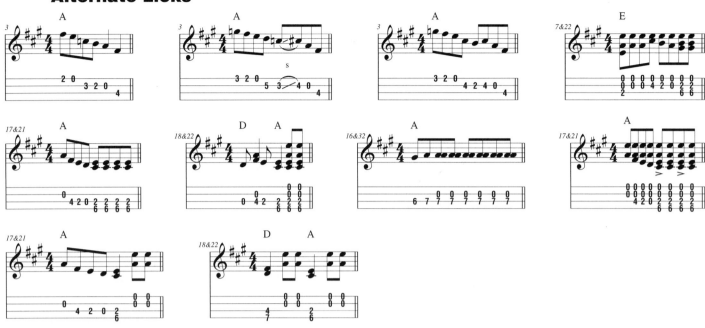

Version 5: Fiddle Style

This version uses scale-based fiddle licks and patterns commonly adapted to the mandolin. As opposed to Bill Monroe's penchant for using pentatonic scales, the following arrangement uses the full, seven-note major scale—in this case, A major. This tune consists of a basic I–IV–V chord progression (A–D–E), so the soloist has a lot of freedom to experiment with chromatic tones, arpeggios, and interesting rhythms—all exemplified in this version (the alternate licks section offers more advanced ideas).

TRACK 40

Key of A

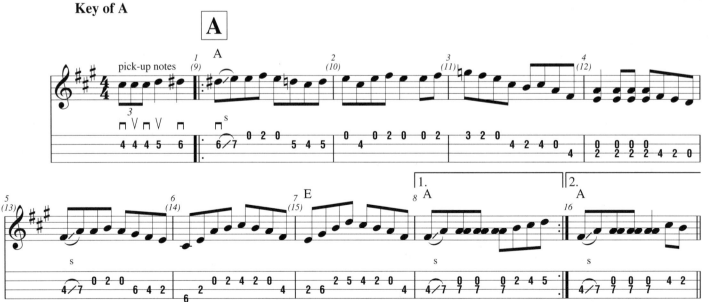

Alternate Licks

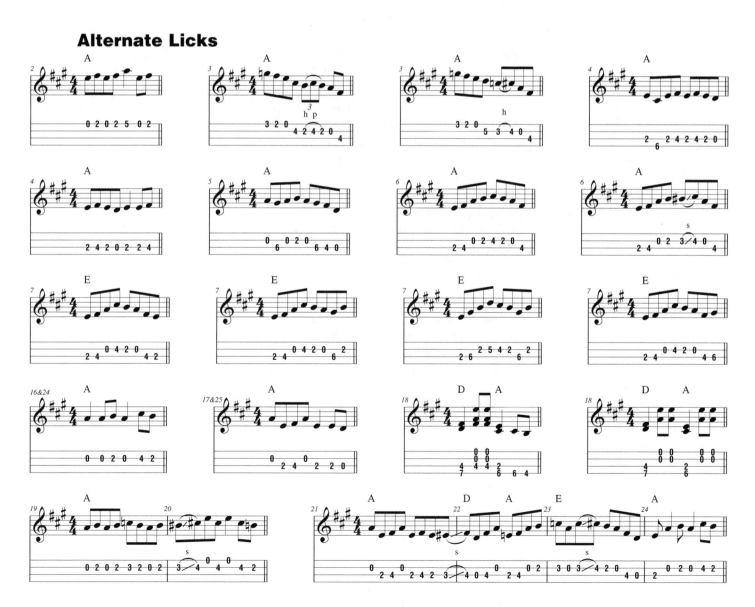

GREAT BALLS OF FIRE

Words and Music by Otis Blackwell and Jack Hammer

Otis Blackwell played a tremendous role in the shaping of rock 'n' roll music in the 1950s. His compositions include "Don't Be Cruel," "All Shook Up," "Fever," "Return to Sender," "Whole Lot a Shakin'," and many other well-known songs during this time period. He wrote hit tunes performed by Elvis Presley, Jerry Lee Lewis, Peggy Lee, and even the Who. In 1955, it is said that he sold several of his demos for $25.00 each, including "Don't Be Cruel." Jerry Lee Lewis went to the top of the charts with "Great Balls of Fire" in 1957.

Rock 'n' roll tunes are often easily adaptable to bluegrass mandolin styles. This tune is a great example of how naturally it fits the mandolin and how much fun it can be to play. Audiences really get excited when they hear this tune performed on a mandolin. Sam Bush, with the Newgrass Revival, was among the first mandolin players known to have recorded this tune in the late 1970s.

The following versions are arranged in a fairly traditional bluegrass style. The tempo should match that of a rock 'n' roll band—with plenty of energy. Version 1 uses recognizable bluegrass licks, many of which are based on the G run. Version 2 builds on this using fiddle-style licks and patterns. Look for the patterns by chord as you work through these, and watch the timing. It will be difficult to keep a straight face when playing "Great Balls of Fire." It is full of fun and energy!

Verse:
You shake my nerves and you rattle my brain
Too much love drives a man insane
You broke my will, but what a thrill
Goodness, gracious, great balls of fire!!

I laughed at love 'cause I thought it was funny
You came along and moooooved me honey
I've changed my mind, this love is fine
Goodness, gracious, great balls of fire!!

Bridge:
Kiss me baby, wooo feels good
Hold me baby, wellllll I want to love you like a lover should
You're fine, sooo kind
I want to tell this world that you're mine, mine, mine, mine

Verse:
I chew my nails and I twiddle my thumbs
I'm real nervous, but it sure is fun
C'mon baby, drive me crazy
Goodness, gracious, great balls of fire!!

Version 1: Some Like It Hot!

This version should be played with plenty of energy! The actual notes help add drive, so it doesn't need to be played at a breakdown tempo to be effective. While the chords add tension and excitement, they are optional. The top note is the melody and should be emphasized. When you do play the chords, notice the similarity with the left-hand shapes.

NOTE: This song's form should be fairly easy to follow. After you play the Intro–Verse–Bridge sections, repeat the Verse. The direction **D.S. al Coda** instructs you to return to the Verse (the 𝄋 symbol) and play to measure 62, where the **To Coda** ⊕ sign is. At this point, you jump to the ⊕ **Coda** to complete the tune. (Just follow the measure numbers.)

TRACK 41

Version 1: Some Like It Hot! *(cont.)*

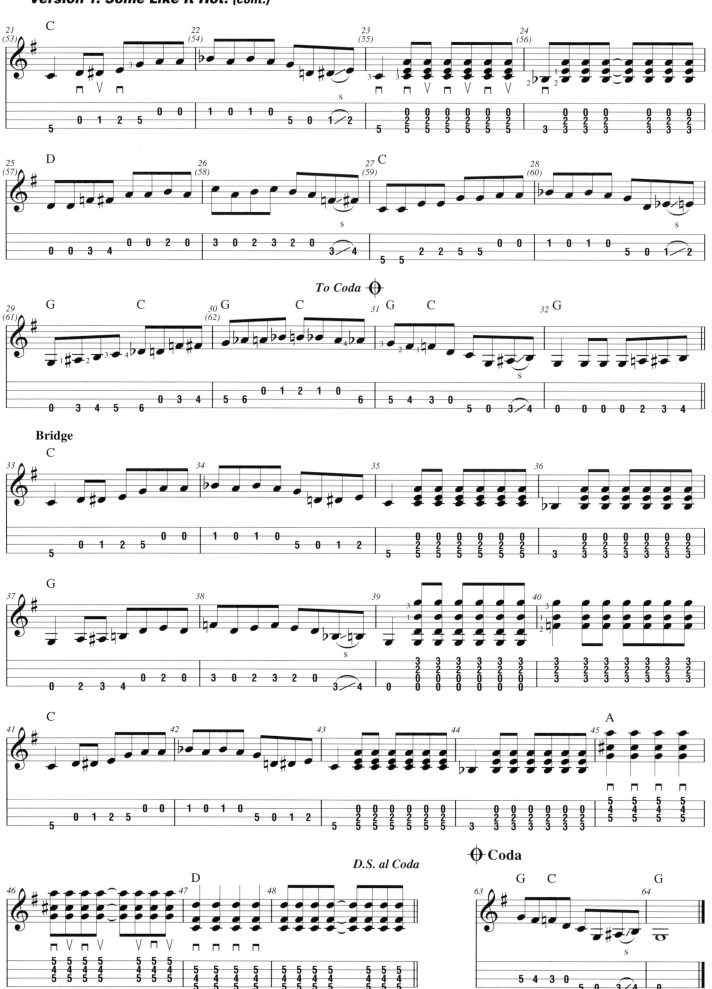

Alternate Intro: measures 1–16

Alternate Licks

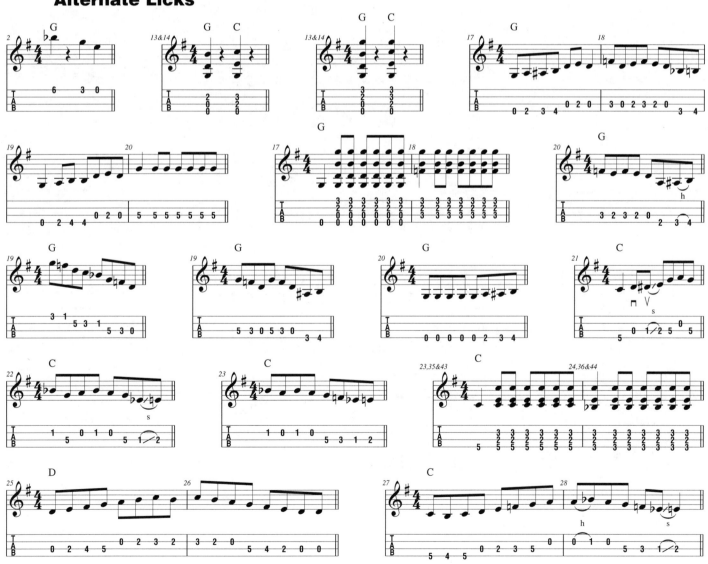

Version 1: Alternate Licks (cont.)

Version 2: Licks on Fire

As you work through this arrangement, compare the patterns by chord to search for common ideas. For example, in the Verse, the lick for the C chord (21–23) is the exact same fingering as the G chord (17–19), but down a string. Realizing these types of similarities will accelerate the learning process.

TRACK 42

Version 2: Licks on Fire (cont.)

Alternate Licks

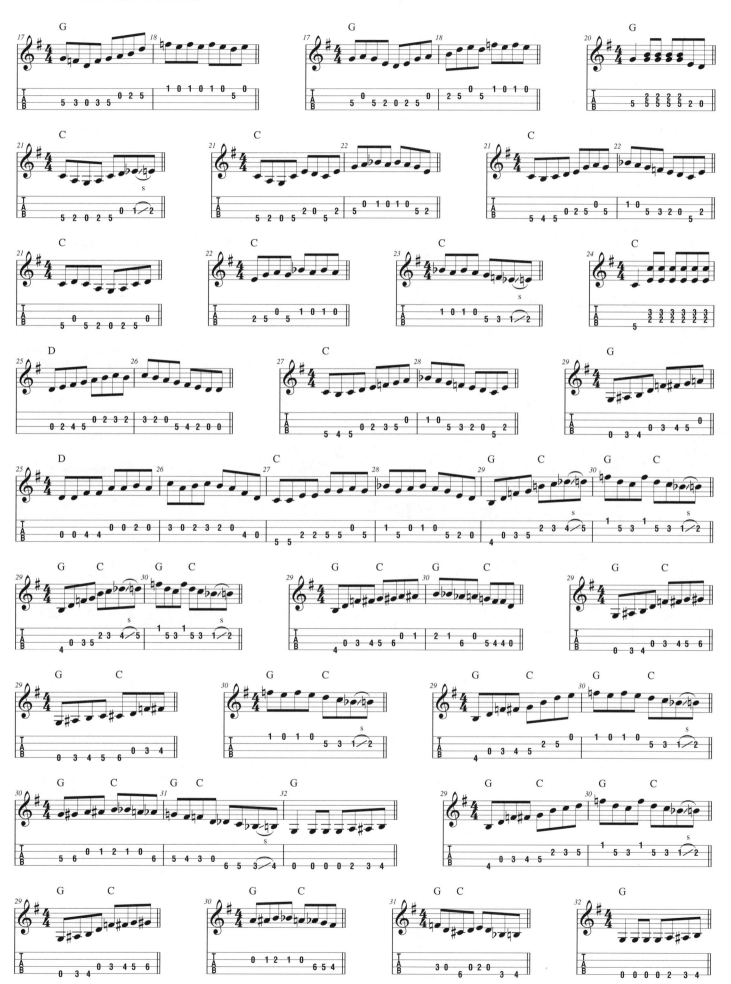

Version 2: Alternate Licks (cont.)

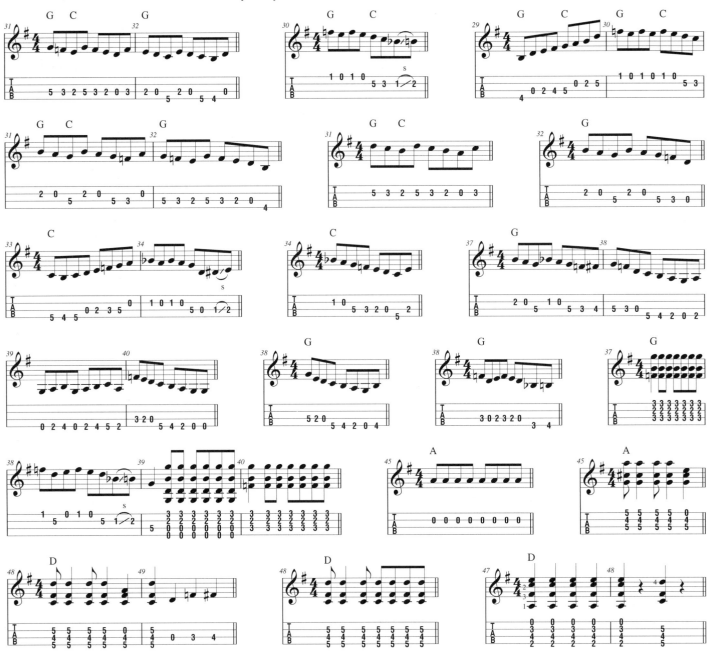

HOW GREAT THOU ART

Words by Stuart K. Hine
Swedish Folk Melody adapted by Stuart K. Hine

In 1885, a Swedish preacher by the name of Carl Boberg, at age 26, wrote the words only of a poem entitled, "O Store Gud." Boberg's poem was published in 1886. Several years later, Boberg attended a meeting and was surprised to hear his poem being sung to the tune of an old Swedish melody.

In the early 1920s, English missionaries, Mr. Stuart K. Hine and his wife, ministered in Poland. It was there they learned the Russian version of Boberg's poem, "O Store Gud," coupled with the original Swedish melody. Later, under inspiration, Stuart K. Hine wrote original English words and made his own arrangement of the Swedish melody, which became popular and is now known as the hymn, "How Great Thou Art."

The first three verses were inspired, line upon line, amidst unforgettable experiences in the Carpathian Mountains. In a village to which he had climbed, Mr. Hine stood in the street singing a gospel hymn and reading aloud "John, Chapter Three." Among the sympathetic listeners was a local village schoolmaster. A storm was gathering, and when it was evident that no further travel could be made that night, the friendly schoolmaster offered his hospitality. Awe-inspiring was the mighty thunder echoing through the mountains, and it was this impression that was to bring about the birth of the first verse.

Pushing on, Mr. Hine crossed the mountain frontier into Romania and into Bukovina. Together with some young people, through the woods and forest glades he wandered and heard the birds sing sweetly in the trees. Thus, the second verse came into being. Verse three was inspired through the conversion of many of the Carpathian mountain-dwellers. The fourth verse did not come about until Mr. Hine's return to Britain.

Oh Lord my God when I in awesome wonder
Consider all the worlds Thy hands have made
I see the stars, I hear the rolling thunder
Thy power throughout the universe displayed

Chorus:
Then sings my soul my Savior God to Thee
How Great Thou Art
How Great Thou Art
Then sings my soul my Savior God to Thee
How Great Thou Art
How Great Thou Art!

When thro' the woods and forest glades I wander
And hear the birds sing sweetly in the trees
When I look down from lofty mountain grandeur
And hear the brook and feel the gentle breeze

Chorus

And when I think that God His Son not sparing
Sent Him to die I scarce can take it in
That on the cross my burden gladly bearing
He bled and died to take away my sin

Chorus

When Christ shall come
With shout of acclamation
And take me home
What joy shall fill my heart
Then I shall bow in humble adoration
And there proclaim my God How Great Thou Art

Chorus

Version 1: Melody in the Key of D

To play gospel tunes, it is helpful to understand that the melodic accents do not always happen on the first beat of each measure. For example, in measure 2, the emphasis is on the third beat. Play this without the tremolo first, in order to place each note on the correct beat. Be careful to hold each note the correct number of beats, i.e. **measure 1:** ♩. = ♩ ♩ ♩ (3 beats).

TRACK 43

Alternate Licks

NOTE: To play along with a hymnal, each two measures of these mandolin arrangements equals one measure in most hymnals.

Transposing

To move the melody to a different key, simply play the exact same position you would in the key of D, but move it up or down a string. Below are the first five measures of "How Great Thou Art" in the keys of G and A, respectively. The key of G is moved down a string, and the key of A is up a string.

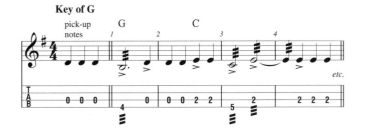

Version 2: Adding Harmony in the Key of D

This version adds harmony notes to the original melody. Optional chords are indicated in parentheses. If the double stop slows the flow of your performance, omit the lower note, because the top is the main melody.

TRACK 44

Alternate Licks

Version 3: Key of D in Triplet Feel

This arrangement uses a special technique where double stops are picked one note at a time instead of simultaneously (hold both notes with the left hand). See the alternate licks for simpler ideas should a measure be too difficult. You can alternate the pick direction throughout, or use the suggested ones to bring out the melody.

Each group of notes is called a *triplet*, which consists of three notes that should be evenly spaced with an accent on the first note. When a rest occurs, leave a space (silence) to keep your timing accurate. Notice that in 4/4 there are four sets of triplets in each measure. Each triplet equals one beat. The three notes of the triplet are played in the same amount of time as one quarter note. As you play each triplet, say "tri-po-let."

TRACK 45

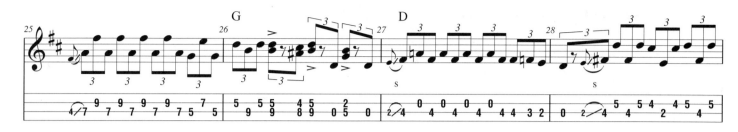

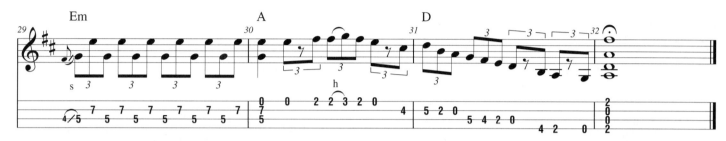

Alternate Licks

Version 3: Alternate Licks *(cont.)*

Version 4: Melody and Harmony in the Key of G

This is arranged in the key of G with the melody notes on the higher strings, and makes a nice contrast with Version 1, which is played in the key of D (substitute these pick-up notes in measure 32 of Version 1 to combine the arrangements). This version also transposes very simply to the key of C (move down one string and play the same fret positions). Left-hand fingerings are suggested below to make this easier to play.

TRACK 46

Key of G

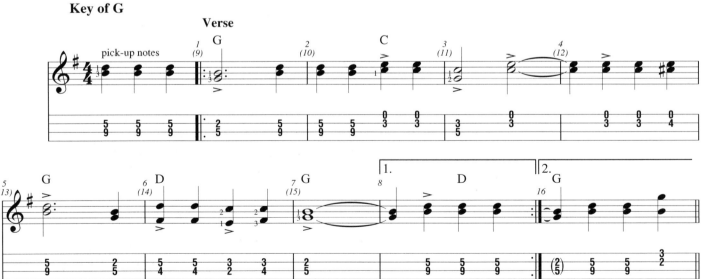

Alternate Licks

Measures 33–35 serve as an optional ending to be played after measure 32.

JERUSALEM'S RIDGE

Words and Music by Bill Monroe

"Jerusalem's Ridge" is a popular fiddle tune composed by Bill Monroe in the key of A minor.

He wrote this tune during a later time in his musical life, well after the folk era of the 1960s, when his newly-composed tunes seemed to include more instrumentals. Originally performed as a mandolin and fiddle tune, "Jerusalem Ridge" has become a standard bluegrass instrumental popular among banjo, guitar, and Dobro® players.

The first version is arranged in the Monroe style, which uses the A minor pentatonic scale (A–C–D–E–G) as the basis for the entire arrangement. The second version is a fiddle-style arrangement based on the seven-note A minor scale (A–B–C–D–E–F–G). Notice that this scale adds two notes to the A minor pentatonic scale used in Version 1 (B and F). This scale, played along one string, uses the following fret distances: 2–1–2–2–1–2–2. This is the fretboard pattern for any natural minor scale starting on its root.

This tune is divided into four sections (Sections D and E are combined as one), each of which is repeated before going on to the next section. It is often helpful to learn a song by working through one section at a time. Several measures of 2/4 time occur in this song, each containing two beats instead of four. Simply play through these without pausing.

For back-up in both versions, the E chord is played as an E *major* chord instead of the naturally-occurring E *minor* chord. This is common for songs played in a minor key because, after Bach's time, people grew used to the powerful sound of the major V chord, whose function is to drive the music back home to the tonic chord (i) of the key. This is actually the reason the *harmonic minor scale* (minor scale with a natural 7th) was developed—so the V chord would naturally be formed with the scale tones as a major chord. It is interesting, when looking at the chord symbols, to notice that Bill Monroe did include the E minor chord right before the final E chord of the song. In mountain modal music, the older version would use only the Em chord.

TRACK 47

Version 1: Monroe Style

Alternate Licks

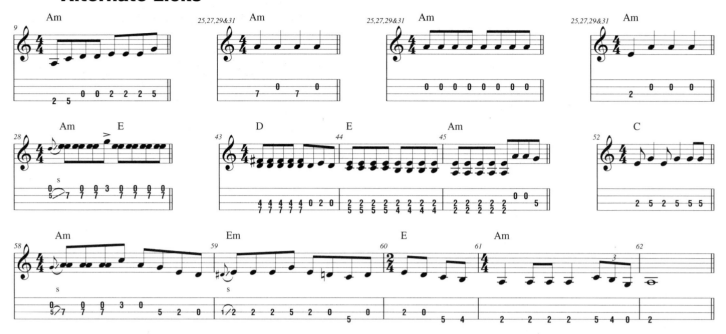

Version 2: Fiddle Style

As compared to the Monroe style, this version is based on the seven-note A natural minor scale, as opposed to the five-note A minor pentatonic scale. For fun, compare the two versions.

TRACK 48

Key of A minor

Alternate Licks

As you play through these lick suggestions, decide whether the style fits the Monroe or fiddle style the best.

Alternate Licks for All Versions by Section

NOTE: Measures which are consecutive, without a space separating them, should work together.

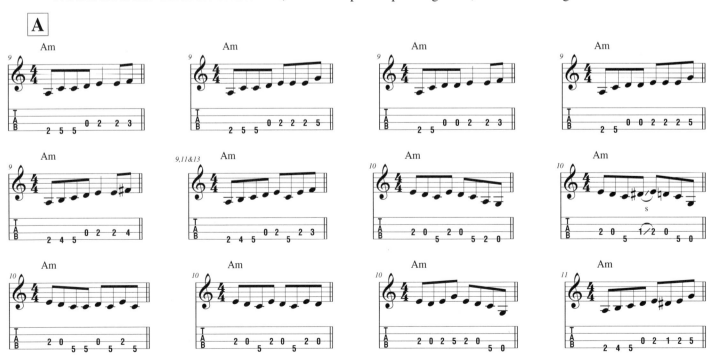

Alternate Licks for All Versions by Section (cont.)

LIMEHOUSE BLUES

Words by Douglas Furber   Music by Philip Braham

"Limehouse Blues" was written during an era when adding the word "blues" to the song title seemed to be in vogue—i.e., "Memphis Blues" (1917), "St. Louis Blues" (1914), "Basin Street Blues" (1928), etc. This jazz standard was composed in the New Orleans jazz style, rather than as a traditional 12-bar blues. This song has continued to be popular through the ever-changing generations of music. It has been heavily performed by jazz musicians, big swing bands, acoustic musicians, and bluegrass musicians as well. "Limehouse Blues" is fun to play on the mandolin. Outstanding acoustic musicians who have recorded this tune include Ronnie Reno, Jethro Burns, Mark O'Connor, Norman Blake, Red Rector, and, of course, Django Reinhardt with Stephen Grappelli on fiddle, who popularized this as a gypsy jazz tune.

"Limehouse Blues" is performed on the mandolin as an instrumental. With blues and jazz in its roots, notice that seventh chords work well as back-up for every chord in this song. They add color and enhance the "bluesy" effect along with the syncopated rhythms. Ninth chords are also effective and provide a more progressive jazz feel. Notice that the main melody notes avoid the root note of the back-up chord. This is also a stylistic feature of jazz music.

The first version for "Limehouse Blues" is arranged in the tremolo style that was used to play the first version for "Alabama Jubilee," "Dear Old Dixie," etc. This arrangement strongly establishes the melody throughout the entire version. Notice that there is natural syncopation in the placement of the melody notes. The second version takes the melody an octave higher.

Version 3 deviates from the melody in an improvisatory fashion. Do you recognize the motif used in measures 13–14 on the A chord? Quoting a brief melodic segment from another tune is a popular technique used in jazz tunes from this era. The second half of the arrangement re-establishes the melody so the audience can continue to relate to the actual song being played.

Versions 4 and 5 present fairly advanced jazz-style arrangements that deviate totally from the melody. They instead work scale passages with and against the chords. They use a variety of rhythms and often include the 9th degree to enhance the jazz-like color. The V chord is often played as an augmented chord in jazz arrangements to increase the tension.

Notice that in the jazz versions, despite the drastic harmonic changes, there are areas where the listener can tell, without a doubt, that it is "Limehouse Blues."

Version 1: Tremolo Style

To start with, play the notes slowly without the use of the tremolo until you "feel" the melody. The effectiveness of tremolo for this version is quite apparent, so do your best to get the technique down. Although this song is in the key of G, don't be thrown by it starting on C (the IV chord).

NOTE: Remember to sustain the half note through two beats: ♩ = ♩͜♩ **(2 beats)** and the whole note through four beats: o = ♩͜♩͜♩͜♩ **(4 beats)**.

TRACK 49

Version 1: Tremolo Style *(cont.)*

Alternate Licks

Version 2: Up-the-Neck

Here we have the melody played an octave higher than Version 1. Embellishment is added throughout to give this a jazzier effect. Tremolo may be played throughout or omitted as you prefer, for example, omit the tremolo in measure 3. For the correct melody placement, play without the tremolo first.

TRACK 50

Key of G

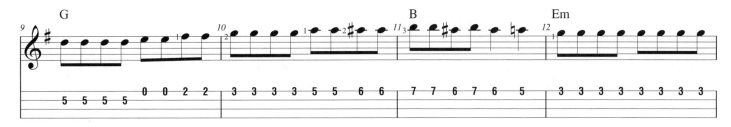

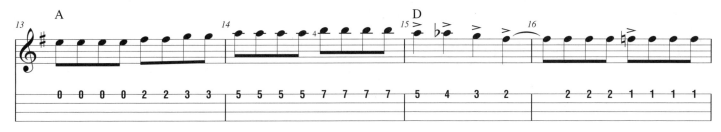

Version 2: Up-the-Neck *(cont.)*

Alternate Licks

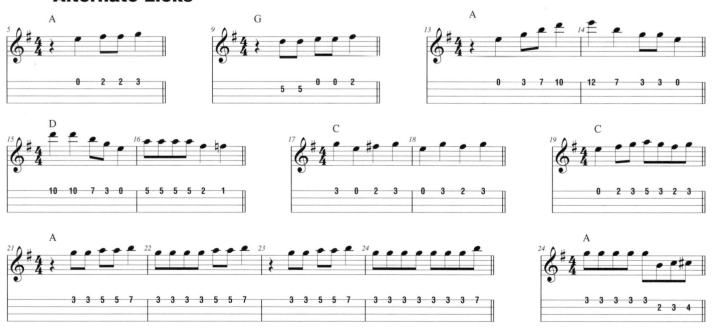

Version 3: Circular Scales and Blue Notes

This arrangement draws from the alternate licks sections. The use of the ♭3rd and ♭7th provide a bluesy effect, while the repeated licks allude to jazz ideas.

TRACK 51

Key of G

Version 3: Circular Scales and Blue Notes *(cont.)*

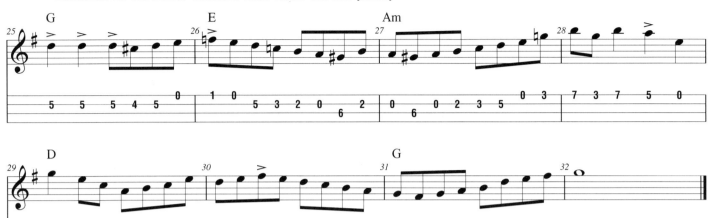

Alternate Licks

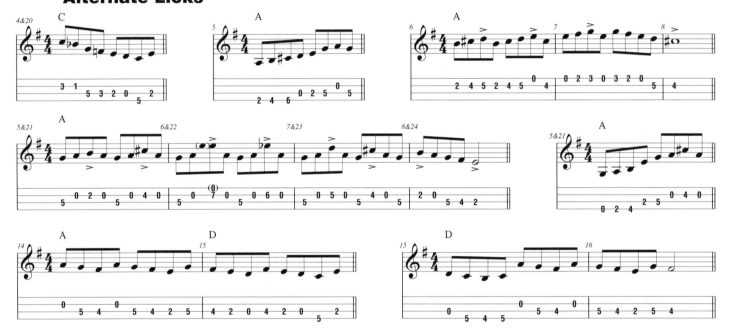

Version 4: Jazz Style

A popular method of jazz music is playing melodies from recognizable songs in the middle of your improvisations. In this one, just for fun, try to hear the borrowed melodies from "Nola."

TRACK 52

Key of G

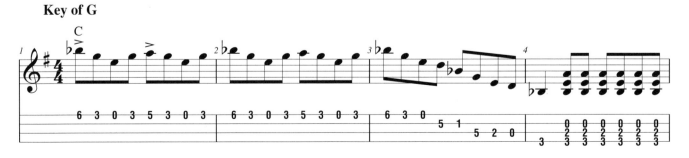

Alternate Licks

Version 5: Jazz-Style Syncopation

Syncopation is very effective for capturing an audience's attention because the expected notes are played on unexpected beats. Notice how the left hand also contributes to the syncopation.

TRACK 53

Key of G

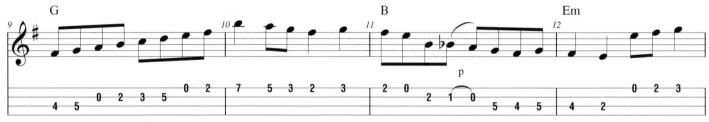

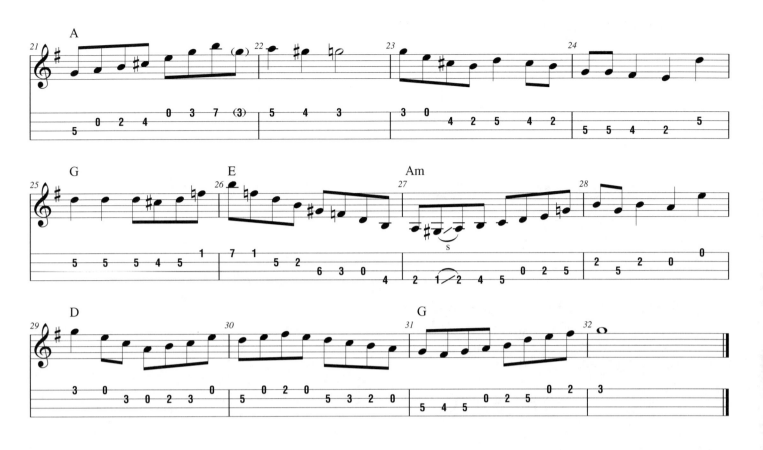

Alternate Licks

Version 5: Alternate Licks (cont.)

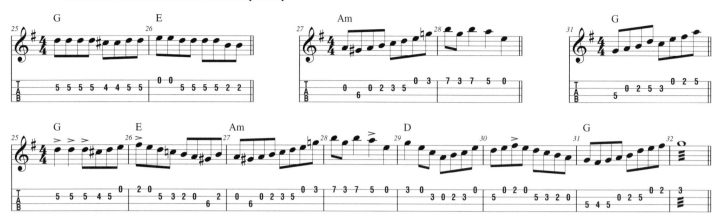

Alternate Licks for All Versions

This tune is a well of wonderful musical ideas, and this section is an effort to offer some of those. Of interest are the alternates for measures 9–12, which quote the melody from "Stumbling," and measures 13–16 from "Nola."

Circular Scale Patterns

NUAGES

By Django Reinhardt and Jacques Larue

Django Reinhardt is considered by many to be among the most influential jazz musicians of all time. Jean-Baptiste "Django" Reinhardt was born on January 23, 1910, into a nomadic gypsy family outside Liberchies in Belgium. (Django, his nickname, is Romani for "I Awake.") His mother was a well-known singer and dancer. Django's first instrument as a child was violin, but he also played banjo, guitar, and a banjo-guitar that had six strings. It is reported that his earliest recordings were of him playing the banjo. At the age of 18, Django was injured in a fire, which devasted his caravan. His right leg was paralyzed, and the ring and pinky fingers of his left hand were badly burned and partially paralyzed. Determined, within a year of extensive therapy, he could walk with a cane. In order to continue playing the guitar, Django miraculously developed an entirely new way to play phenomenal lead and back-up using only two fingers. His two injured fingers could be used for certain chords, which helped to develop and shape an entirely new sound.

Django formed the Quintette du Hot Club de France with the Parisian violinist, Stephane Grappelli. His brother, Joseph, played guitar along with Roger Chaput, and Louis Vola was on bass. This quintet consisted entirely of stringed instruments. Their music was a new sound in jazz, with the acoustic guitars providing the percussion.

"Nuages," which means "clouds" in French, was written and recorded by Django as an instrumental in 1940. Today, this gypsy jazz tune, which is played in the key of G major, is considered the most famous of all of his original compositions. He recorded it 13 different times, each with slight variation. The first recording, in 1940, was performed with the clarinet and played up-tempo. It was not an immediate success. However, as time progressed, during World War II, "Nuages" made it to the top of the Hit Parade in France and Britain. After the war was over, Django reunited with Stephane Grappelli, who had been in England during World War II. They recorded this tune with the Quintet on January 31, 1946. With Django on the acoustic Macceferri guitar and Stephane playing the hauntingly beautiful melody on the violin at a moderately slow tempo, along with the steady back-up rhythms from the Quintet, the recording became a huge success. "Nuages" had fully arrived! Lyrics were also composed in 1946, an introduction was added before the main melody, and sheet music was published for "Nuages" under the title "The Bluest Kind of Blues (My Baby Sings)." Spencer Williams is credited with the lyrics. "The Bluest Kind of Blues" was a popular hit in America as well. Django recorded it six more times before his death in 1953 at the age of 43.

The chords are important components to the beauty and flow of the melody for "Nuages." The chords above the music in the following arrangements offer several options. On top are the basic chords, which are very effective, even without all of the extended jazz chord options. Below these are suggested passing chords, which add rhythm and motion. The third row are additional jazz chords that can be played. Most importantly, the rhythm should be played continuously with the chords providing a steady back-up on each beat.

Version 1: Melody

This version's melody is beautiful and dream-like—reminiscent of "Clair de Lune" by Claude Debussy—when played at a moderately slow tempo. The back-up chords should be played with a straight comping style using block-style chords for a soft, percussive effect.

There are three rows of chords, each representing increasing degrees of harmonic complexity, from high to low: 1) the basic chords used on Django's 1936 record with simpler options in parentheses, 2) adds passing chords, and 3) full jazz extended chords. As always, the chords in parentheses are optional.

TRACK 54

Version 1: Melody (cont.)

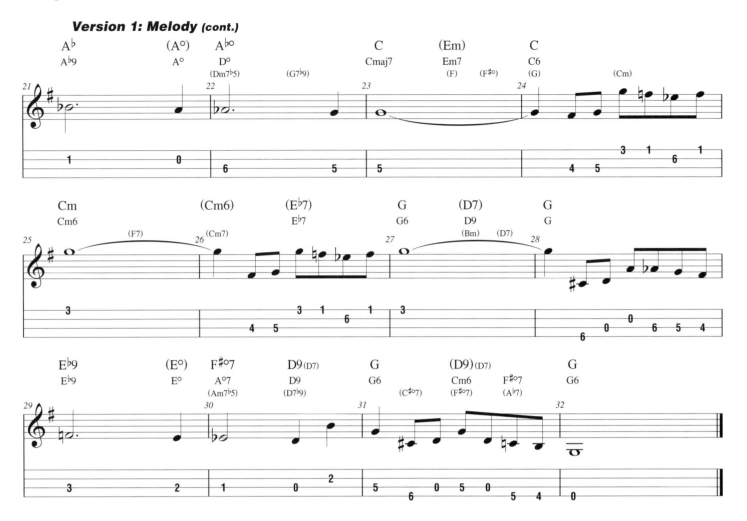

Alternate Licks

These alternate licks will add some swing!

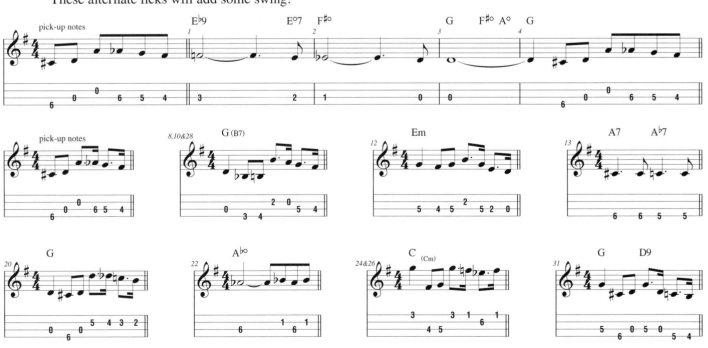

Version 2: Melody an Octave Higher

This version is identical to Version 1, except it is played an octave higher.

Version 2: Melody an Octave Higher *(cont.)*

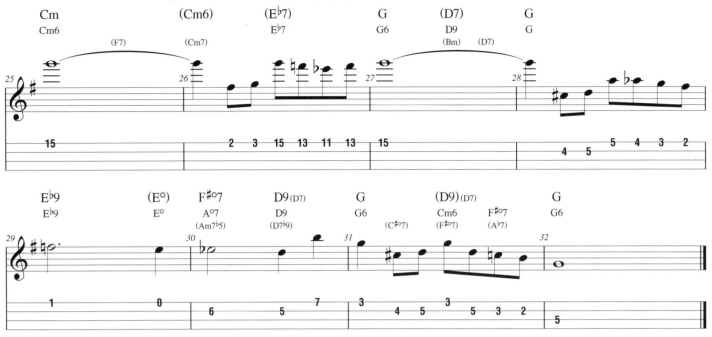

Alternate Licks

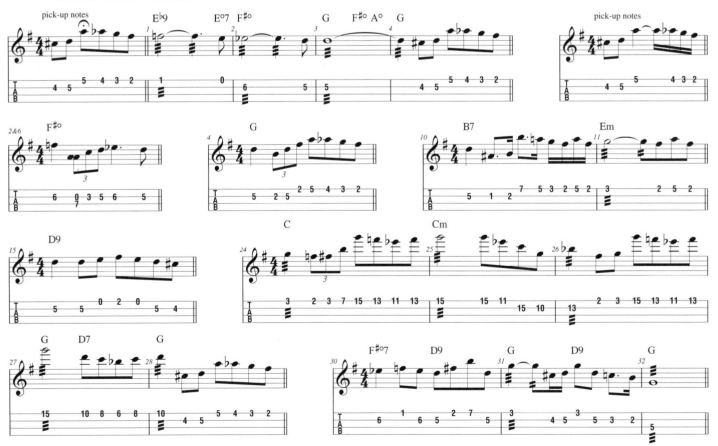

ORANGE BLOSSOM SPECIAL

Words and Music Ervin T. Rouse

Possibly the most famous fiddle tune of all time, "Orange Blossom Special" is also easily recognizable as a true bluegrass classic. The origin for the tune is somewhat controversial. At a Kerrville Bluegrass Festival in Texas during the late 1970s, Chubby Wise expressed his side of the story in a concert where I was present. He described how he and Ervin Rouse had composed the tune together in Florida. When they parted, Ervin expressed that he thought the song had a future. Chubby told him to do whatever he wished with it. "Orange Blossom Special" was copyrighted with Ervin T. Rouse receiving the credit. The actual copyright date, however, is reported to have been a month before this meeting was supposed to have taken place. Today, many people credit Chubby Wise and Ervin Rouse as the original composers of the music. Others say it is possible that Chubby worked with Ervin on an earlier similar tune. In any case, it is well-known that Chubby Wise did much throughout the years to promote and popularize "Orange Blossom Special," though Ervin Rouse officially composed this tune.*

The song was written about a passenger train, the *Orange Blossom*, which ran between Florida and New York from about 1925 to 1952. As the song progresses, the listener can almost feel the wheels turning and the engine whirring.

A discography of artists who have recorded this song would be a very long list. Among these are Bill Monroe, Johnny Cash (who helped to popularize the words written by Ervin's brother, Jack Rouse), Charlie McCoy, the Nitty Gritty Dirt Band, the Stanley Brothers, Bob Wills, Chet Atkins, Flatt and Scruggs, Country Gentlemen, Roy Clark, Carl Jackson, Benny Martin, Scotty Stoneman, Mark O'Connor, the Osborne Brothers, and many more.

Originally written for the fiddle, "Orange Blossom Special" is also a natural for the mandolin and a great crowd pleaser. The tune begins with a tension-mounting introduction on a single chord (the V chord). A surge of energy moves the Intro into Section A on the home chord of the key (I). Right after Section B is completed, this procedure is repeated. The three sections are played over and over until the artist finally decides to end the song. This tune is traditionally played in the key of A. Four arrangements are presented here in the order of difficulty. Learn these one at a time, then combine them as you please. Also, create your own arrangement(s) by combining your favorite sections from each arrangement, and by using the alternate licks.

Look a-yonder comin'
Comin' down that railroad track
Hey, look a-yonder comin'
Comin' down that railroad track
It's the Orange Blossom Special
Bringin' my baby back
Well, I'm going down to Florida
And get some sand in my shoes
Or maybe Californy
And get some sand in my shoes
I'll ride that Orange Blossom Special
And lose these New York blues
"Say man, when you going back to Florida?"

"When am I goin' back to Florida?
I don't know, don't reckon I ever will."
"Ain't you worried about getting your
Nourishment in New York?"
"Well, I don't care if I
Do-die-do-die-do-die-do-die."
Hey talk about a-ramblin'
She's the fastest train on the line
Talk about a-travellin'
She's the fastest train on the line
It's that Orange Blossom Special
Rollin' down the seaboard line

* Recommended Reading: Book/CD *Orange Blossom Boys* by Randy Noles, with forewords by John Hartford and Marty Stuart—the "untold" story with a CD, which alternates between interviews and how "Orange Blossom Special" has been played (HL00000282).

Version 1: Bluegrass

In the key of A, this song starts on the E chord (V chord). This creates a lot of tension, exciting the audience when the A chord finally comes. Section A can be played with tremolo or as written. Section B is an interesting change of melodic ideas based in the key of A major, finally establishing its tonality. Measures 61–65 serve as an ending where the tempo gradually slows (*rit.*).

TRACK 55

Repeat or End

Alternate Licks

Here are the alternate licks presented by sections. Section A is mainly chordal, while Section B is more
melodic.

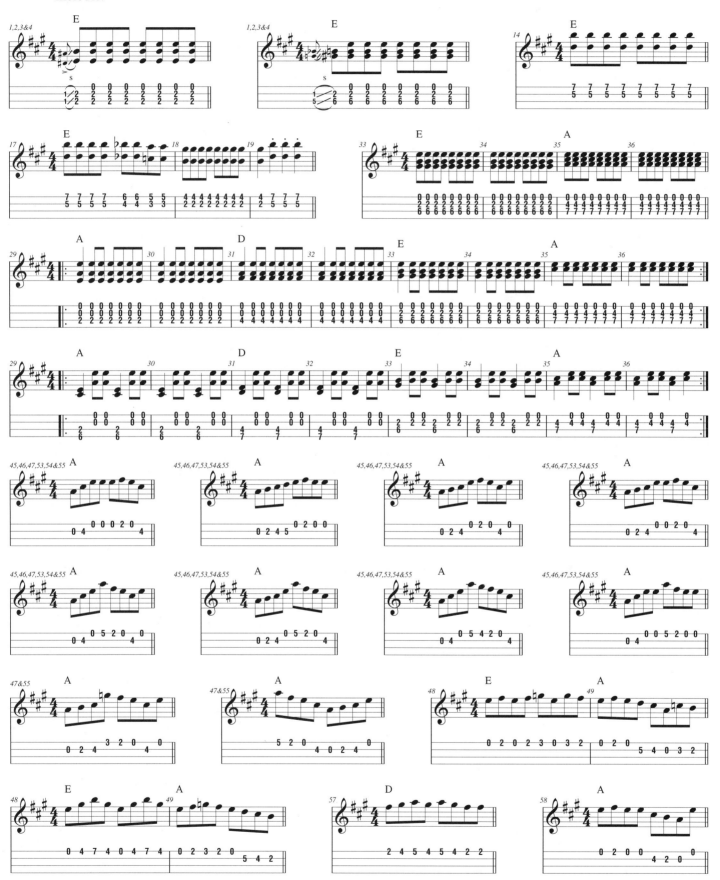

Version 2: Adding Harmony Notes

This builds on the previous version by adding larger chord voicings and more challenging melodic lines. The tremolo and articulations can be changed at your discretion. To make this easy for the left hand, note the similarity of the chord shapes.

TRACK 56

Version 2: Adding Harmony Notes (cont.)

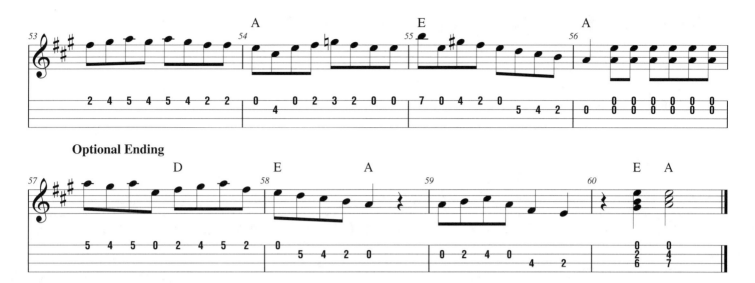

Optional Ending

Alternate Licks

Of particular interest in measures 34 and 38 is the use of the *augmented chord* (a major triad with a raised 5th: 1–3–♯5, indicated with a "+" after the chord name). This may sound strange by itself, but in the song's context, it adds significant dramatic tension.

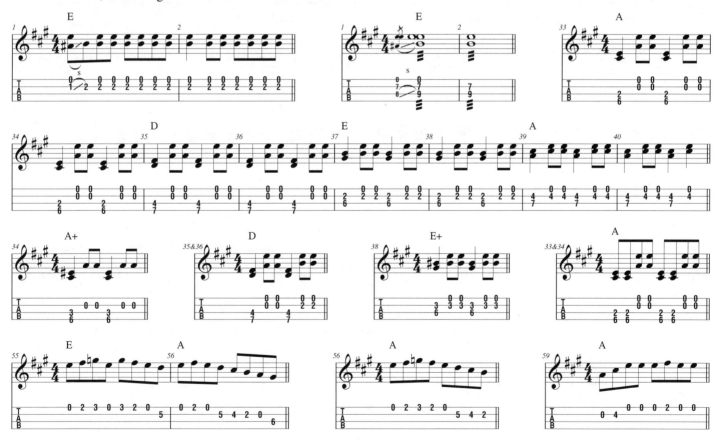

Version 3: Building on Previous Versions

This version builds upon Versions 1–2 and the alternate licks. In Section A, the repeated section is written out to include ideas like augmented chords (measures 42 and 46) and shuffle rhythms used by fiddlers. Section B, which arpeggiates the chord tones, includes suggested left-hand fingerings. Relax your right-hand wrist when strumming the strings.

TRACK 57

Version 3: Building on Previous Versions (cont.)

Alternate Licks

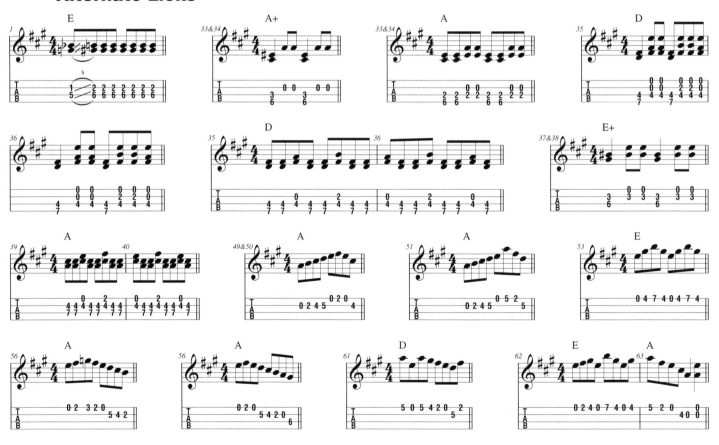

Version 4: Using Slides, Harmonics, Double Shuffle, etc.

The Intro is divided into three sections of 16 measures each. To shorten the Intro, jump directly from measure 24 to 54. Section A is played in the double-shuffle rhythm, so getting that under your fingers is important. Practice playing measures 66 and 67 with the right hand only, to feel the effect, then add the left hand. Emphasize the treble strings every third stroke in this two-measure rhythm pattern. After you play Section B, to complete the tune, fade out with the first four measures of the Intro, then end on the I chord (A).

TRACK 58

Key of A

Version 4: Using Slides, Harmonics, Double Shuffle, etc. (cont.)

Alternate Licks by Section

Section A is offered with three different options (measures 66–73). These also work well as exercises for the double-shuffle rhythms. Keep your wrist relaxed, emphasize the accented notes, and follow the left-hand fingerings and pick directions closely as you play through these. Also, E and A augmented chords make passing-chord appearances. Section B has challenging up-the-neck options, too.

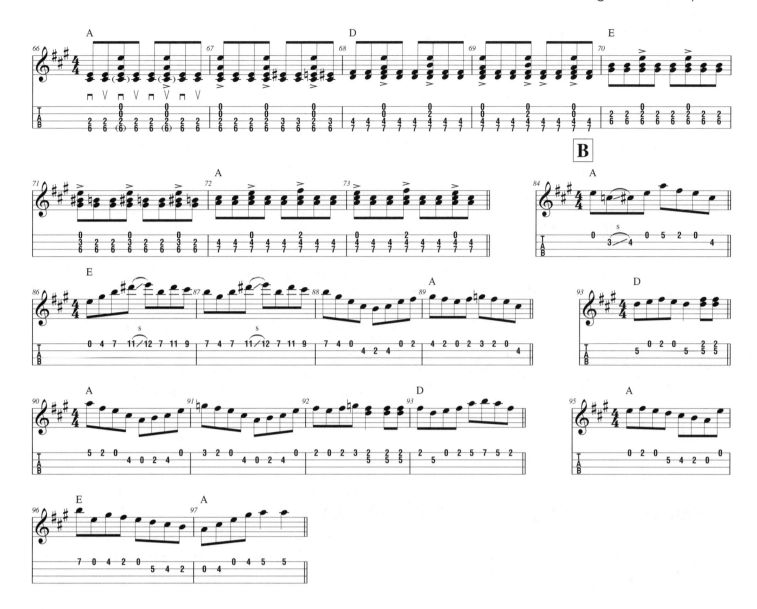

RAWHIDE

Words and Music by Bill Monroe

"Rawhide" is a powerful instrumental bluegrass tune. This was one of the earliest tunes written by Bill Monroe to be played at a very fast tempo. Although not titled as a breakdown, this tune should be performed with a lot of energy at a breakdown tempo.

"Rawhide" is usually thought of as a mandolin instrumental, which is Bill Monroe's main instrument, but all bluegrass musicians and audiences seem to love this tune. It is a song any mandolin player should enjoy playing.

The original LP, *Bluegrass Instrumentals*, lists the title for this song as "Raw Hide" rather than "Rawhide." However, today it appears written either way. This song is said to have been titled after the movie, *Raw Hide*, as Bill Monroe knew the star. However, this should not be confused with Frankie Laine's theme from the television show of the same name, for they are not the same.

Bill Monroe originally released "Rawhide" (with "Letter from My Darlin'" on the flip side) as a 78 in January of 1952. Along with Bill Monroe was Jimmy Martin on guitar, Rudy Lyle on banjo, Joel Price on bass, and Red Taylor on fiddle.

"Rawhide" is traditionally played in the key of C and consists of a Section A (played twice)* and a Bridge section. Traditionally, the mandolin begins Section A in the open-string area and plays up-the-neck for the repeat. The Bridge's chords move along the circle of fifths in a strong rhythmic fashion, heightening the listener's anticipation for what is to come. This part is like a signature section that audiences love. When it has been played, the next instrument takes over, or the mandolin can begin a new variation. To end the song, play the Tag directly after Section A.

*On the audio, Section A is played only one time. However, traditionally, this section is repeated. The ending is also not played on the audio with each version.

Version 1: Traditional Bluegrass

"Rawhide" uses the standard I–IV–V chords (C, F, and G) for Section A. Notice the Monroe-style licks starting at measure 13. The placement of the notes adds drive and motion without increasing the tempo. The Bridge's chord progression is E–A–D–G, following the circle of fifths, and leads smoothly into the C chord of Section A. Finally, notice how most of Section A has two measures per chord, whereas the chords for the Bridge are four measures each. Remember to keep repeating Section A and the Bridge until you're ready to end the tune. Then, play Section A one last time and the ending. The Tag ending is included after Version 1, but not on the audio.

TRACK 59
(Played w/o repeats
or Coda)

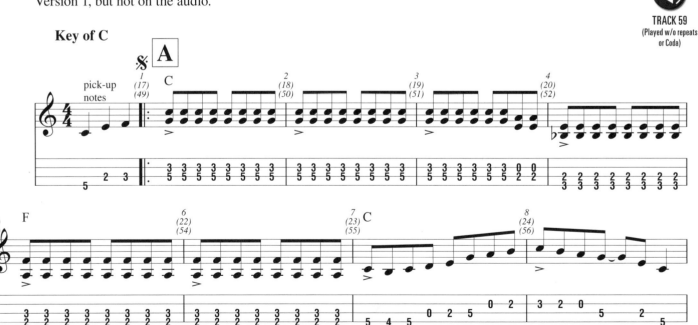

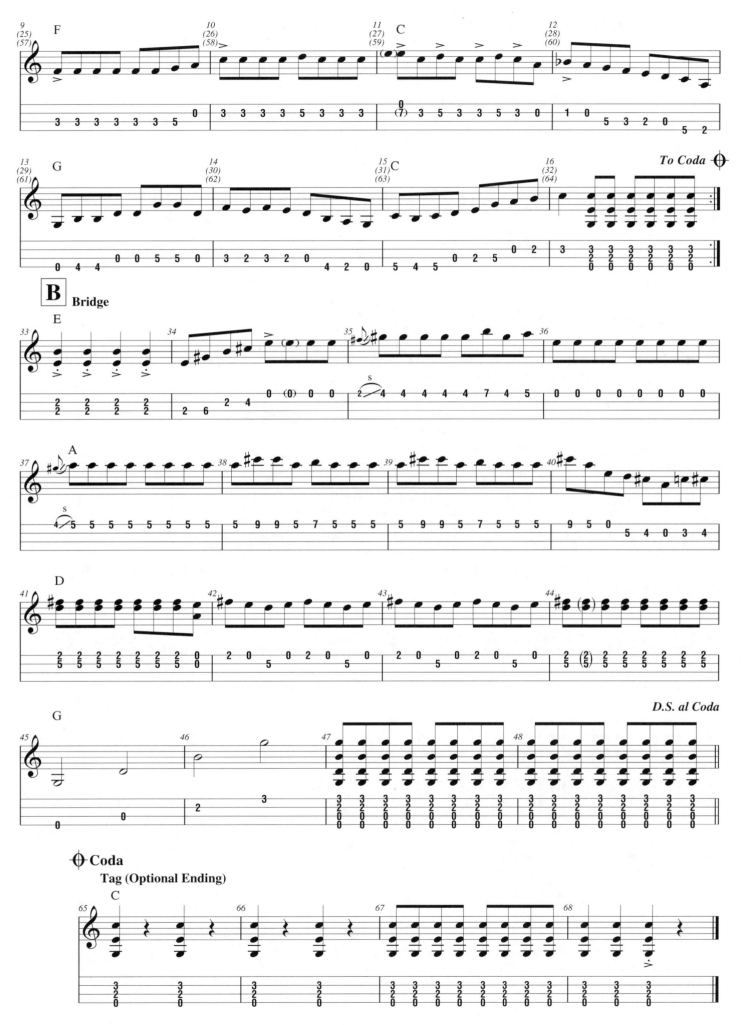

Alternate Licks by Section

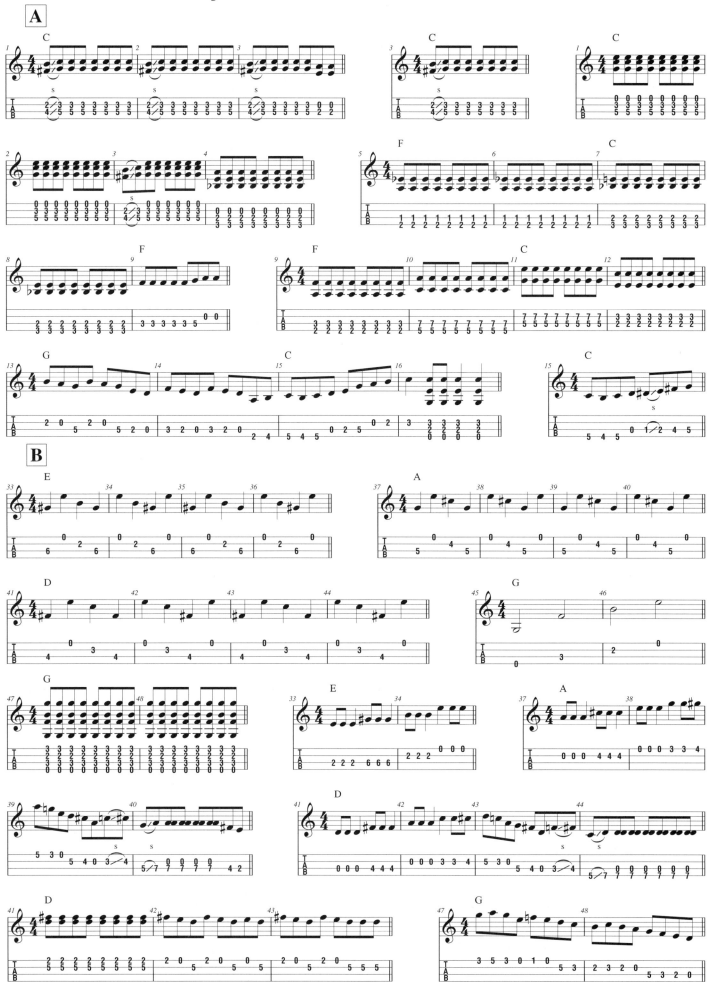

Version 2: Applying Alternate Licks

"Rawhide," like so many other bluegrass tunes, can be varied every time it is played. Many licks work well for each chord, making it a really fun tune to work with. When you repeat Section A in Version 1, you can use any version's Section A as an intriguing variation. The Bridge imitates the banjo from the original recording, which the audience loves because of the driving energy the rhythmic contrast provides.

TRACK 60
(Played w/o repeats or Coda)

Version 2: Applying Alternate Licks (cont.)

Alternate Licks by Section

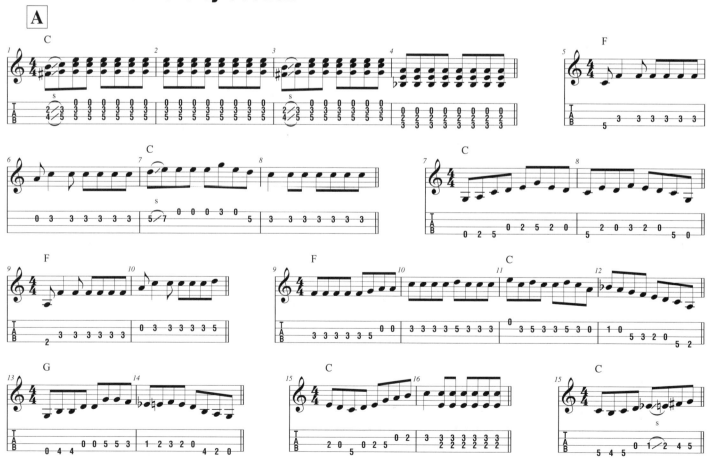

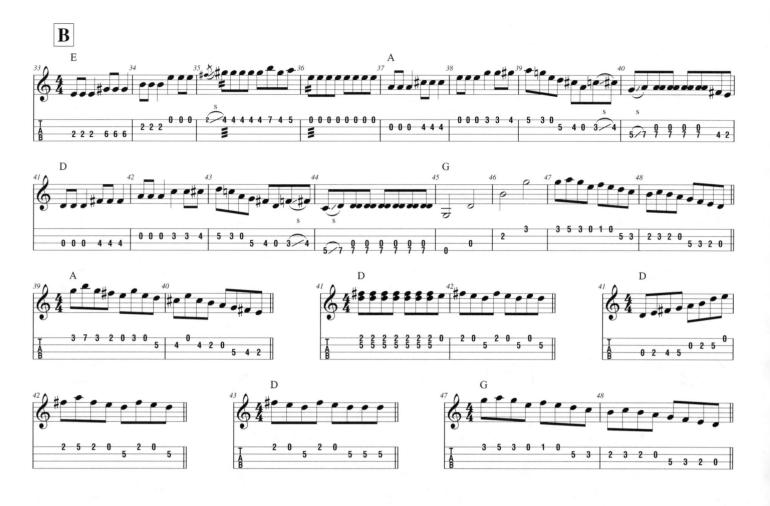

Version 3: Contemporizing the Arrangement

This version builds on the previous ones by adding chromatic tones and syncopated rhythms to suggest a slight jazz flavor.

TRACK 61
(Played w/o repeats
or Coda)

Key of C

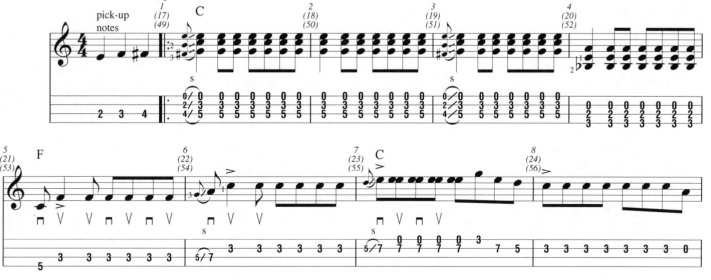

Version 3: Contemporizing the Arrangement (cont.)

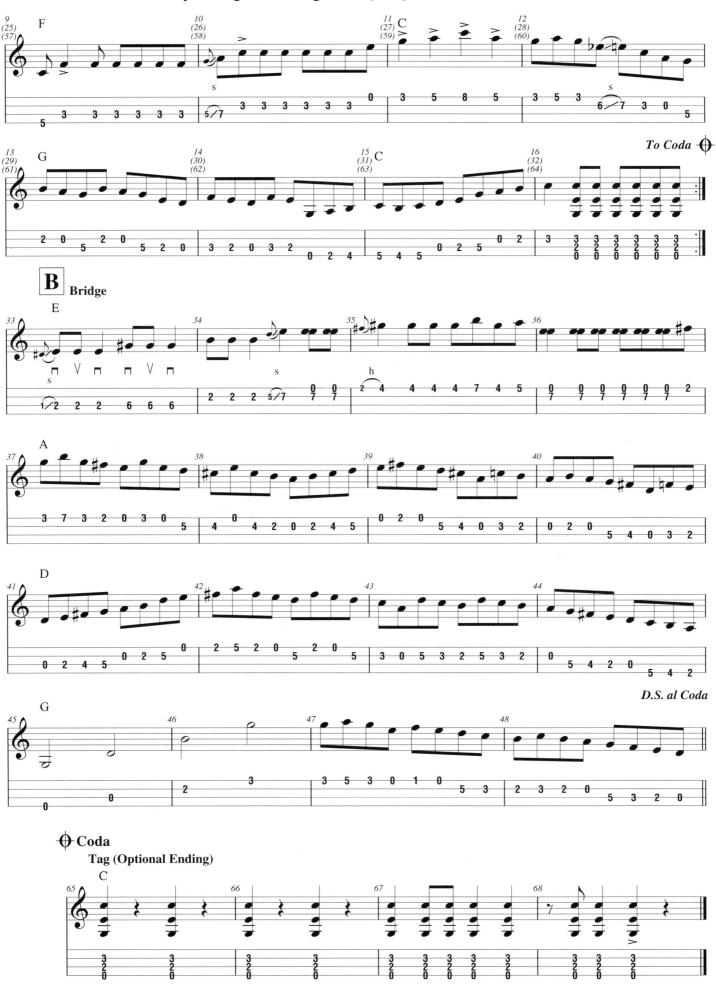

Alternate Licks by Section

Version 4: Up-the-Neck

Pay attention to the left-hand fingering as you work through this. Section A also provides an excellent substitute for Version 1 on the repeat.

TRACK 62
(Played w/o repeats
or Coda)

Key of C

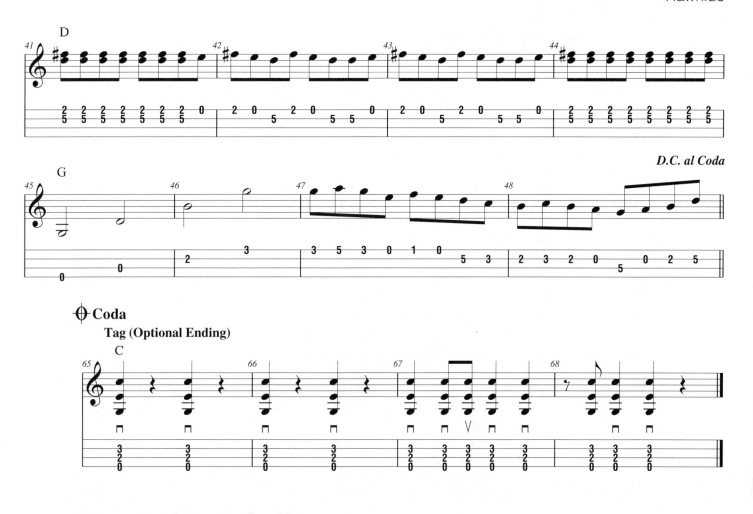

D.C. al Coda

Coda
Tag (Optional Ending)

Alternate Licks by Section

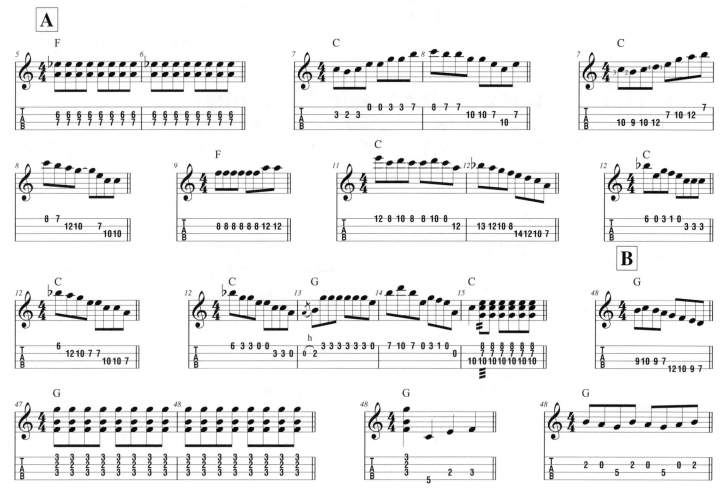

RED WING

Words by Thurland Chattaway   Music by Kerry Mills

"Red Wing" is a classic tune that is easily recognized among people of all ages. Kerry Mills also wrote "Whistling Rufus" (1899) and "Meet Me in St Louis, Louis" (1904), among other recognizable tunes from this era. "Red Wing" is a popular tune to play on just about any instrument. Fiddle players think of this as a fiddle tune, hammered dulcimer players think of it as a hammered dulcimer tune, and, of course, it is a beautiful song when played on the mandolin. The original music was for piano, and it is a popular jam session tune among bluegrass musicians, as well as having often been recorded.

The key of G is common for this tune. The first version provides a strong melody with suggested harmony notes. The second version builds on the first and adds a more flowing feeling. The third version builds on the second version with chromatic and blues tones. This is usually performed by bluegrass musicians as an instrumental and is played at a moderately bouncy tempo.

There once lived an Indian maid
A shy little Indian maid
Who sang a lay, a love song gay
As o'er the plain she'd while the time away
She loved a warrior bold, this shy little maid of old
But blythe and gay he rode one day
To battle far away
Now the moon shines tonight on pretty Red Wing
The breezes sighing, the night birds crying
While far beneath the stars her brave is sleeping
Poor Red Wing weeping her heart away
She watched through the day and night
She kept the campfire bright
While under the sky each night she would lie
And dream about his coming by and by
But when the braves returned
The heart of Red Wing yearned
For brave one day her warrior gay
Fell bravely in the fray

Version 1: Melody with Basic Harmony

The Verse of this version is strictly melody-centered, but the Chorus adds optional harmony notes on the lower strings. The alternate licks section offers, as well as fresh ideas, the Chorus without the harmony notes.

TRACK 63

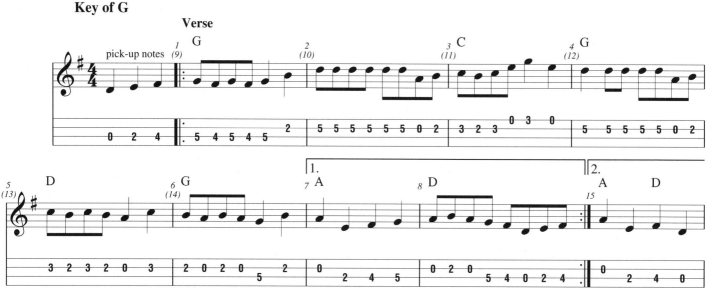

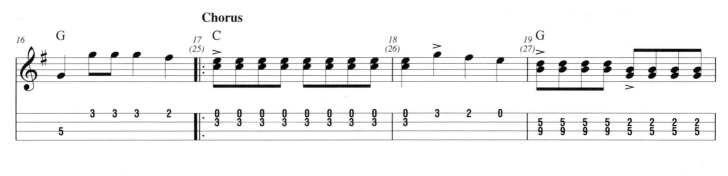

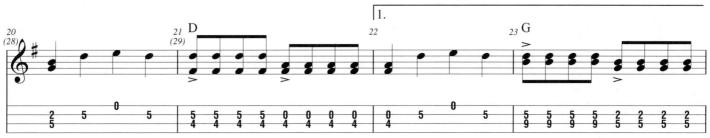

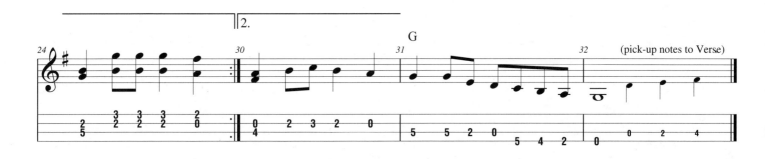

Alternate Licks

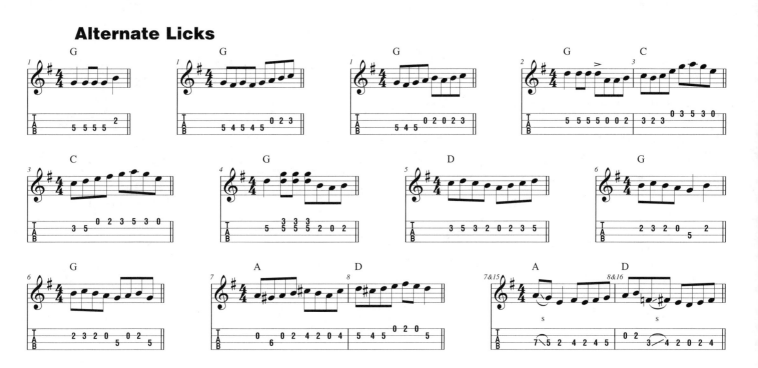

Version 1: Alternate Licks (cont.)

Version 2: Adding Scale Tones and Slides

Left-hand fingerings are included for smoother transitions. To play this in the key of C, move every note down one string and play the same fret numbers (begin on the G string).

TRACK 64

Key of G

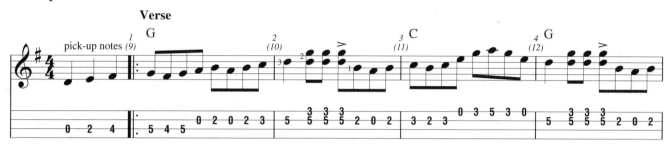

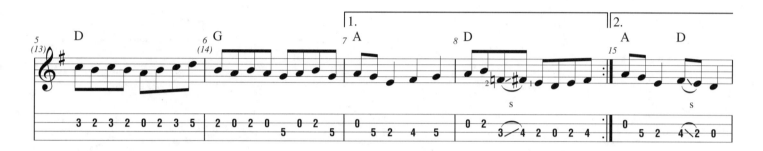

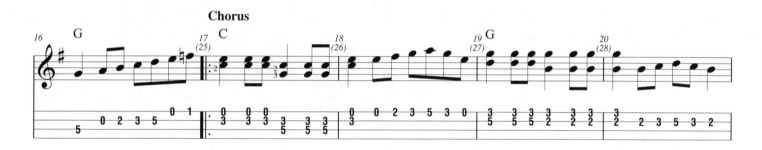

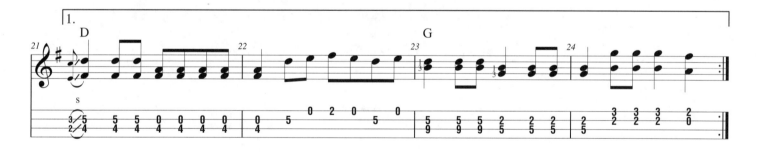

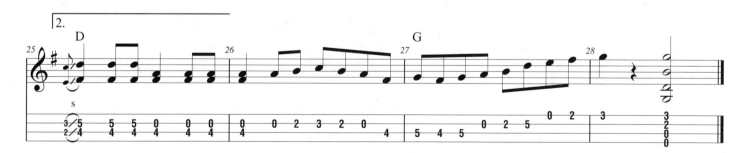

169

Alternate Licks

Version 3: Adding Embellishment

This version embellishes upon Version 2 by adding 7ths and chromatic tones to add motion—especially for the V chord in the V–I chord changes (G–C, D–G, A–D).

Key of G

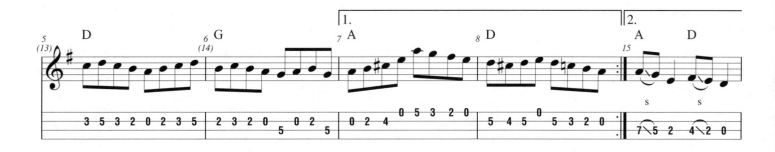

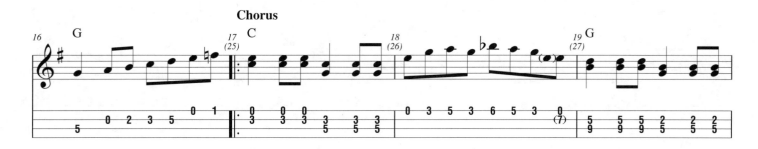

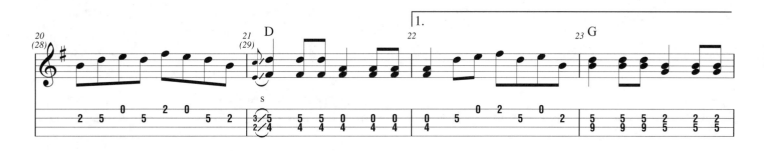

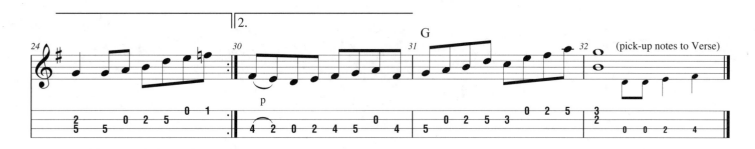

Alternate Licks

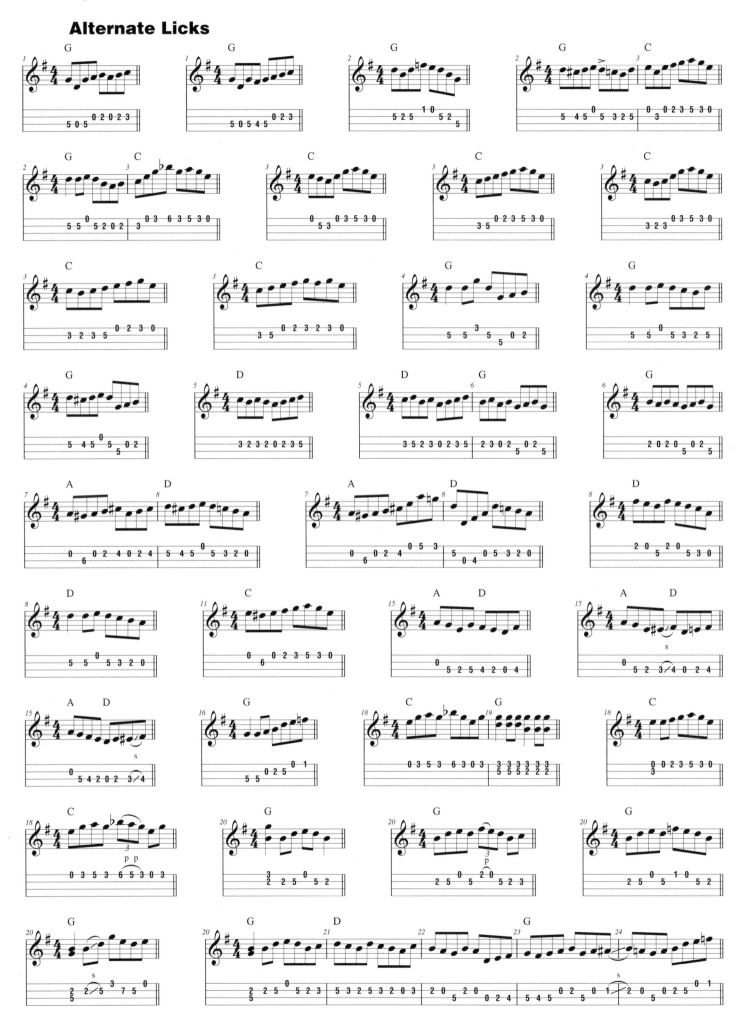

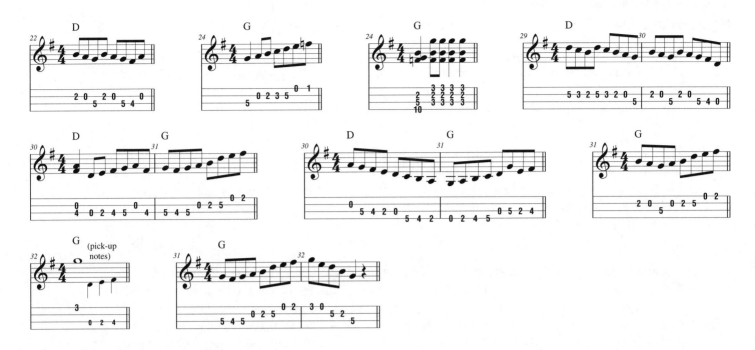

ROANOKE

Music by Joe Ahr

In the 1950s, Bill Monroe composed some of his best-known signature tunes of bluegrass music, including "Uncle Pen," "Wheel Hoss," and "Roanoke" (composed under his pseudonym "Joe Ahr"), which have become favorite "fiddle tunes" among mandolin players. "Roanoke" was first recorded in 1954 with Bill Monroe on mandolin, Hubert Davis on 5-string banjo, and Bobby Hicks and Charlie Cline playing the two fiddles.

The melodic/fiddle style of playing the mandolin is an accepted and very popular way to play fiddle tunes. Essentially, the mandolin plays the same notes that the fiddle plays, picking scale-like passages. This builds on Monroe's own mandolin style, which is a more chordal approach using major pentatonic scales for the runs. Virtually every note in the fiddle style is a melody note. Bill Keith, who played banjo with Bill Monroe in the 1960s, helped develop and popularize this style of playing. Today, this is the standard way to play "Roanoke" among most mandolin players, flatpickers, 5-string banjo players, and Dobro® players.

"Roanoke" is traditionally played in the key of G, but it is fun to realize that the original melody for Section A was built with notes from the G major pentatonic scale, which uses only five notes from the G major scale. The pentatonic scale omits the 4th and 7th degrees of the major scale. The example below is an octave of the G major scale with these tones in parentheses. Practicing the scales will make playing in this style easier and smoother. Compare the notes in Section A with these two scales. Try to identify the sounds that make them different.

G Major Scale

Version 1 Part A: m. 4
Using G Major Scale

Version 1 Part A: m. 4
Using G Pentatonic Scale

The traditional fiddle tune form applies to this tune: A–A–B–B. Notice that Section A is played with the scale-like fiddle-style patterns, and Section B uses a chordal approach. There are so many ways to vary this tune once you have learned the basic version that one should never get bored.

"Roanoke" is also played at a fast tempo. This is never a must, as playing it clearly and cleanly is more effective if a choice must be made.

NOTE: Substitute chords are also indicated in parentheses for the final I–V–I in each section. The swing style back-up most associated with "Gray Eagle" and "Sally Goodin'" also works well with Section A: G–G7–C–C#°–G–G#–Am–D7, etc. Once you have learned the main arrangement, try substituting different ideas from the alternate licks.

Version 1: Standard Version

This version is fun to play, establishes the melody, and includes signature nuances. The original melody for Section A was written from the G major pentatonic scale, but, while artists endeavor to retain that effect, they often include other notes as passing tones.

TRACK 66

Key of G

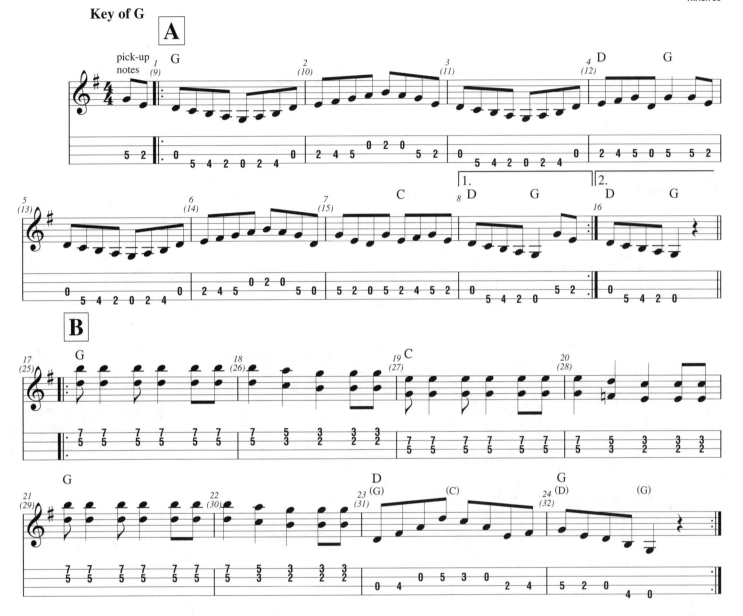

Optional Introductions

Performances of this tune often include a solo Intro. Two options are offered below. Beat 4 of measure 4 contains the pick-up notes to the Verse where the band kicks in. This song can also be played without the Intro. Additionally, if you don't use it as an Intro, it can be played as an ending after Section B.

Alternate Licks for Section A

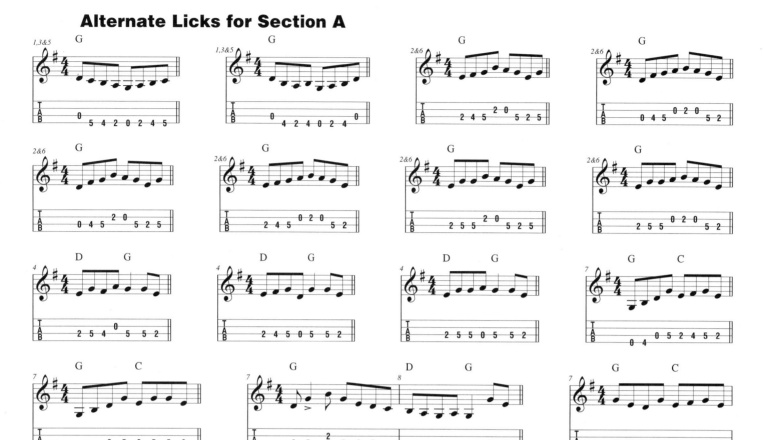

Alternate Section A

The following offers two different treatments for Section A. The first uses all seven notes of the G major scale. The second Section A uses notes from the G major pentatonic scale.

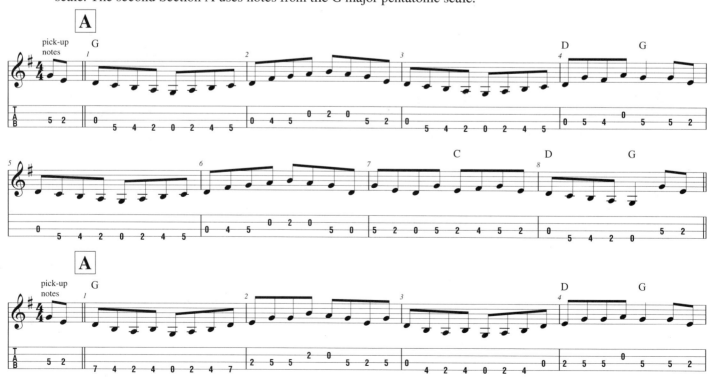

Alternate Licks for Section B

Alternate Section B

These two alternate versions of Section B use longer slide ideas from the previous alternate licks section.

Version 2: Adding Blues and Chromatic Notes

This version serves an effective performance variation by adding chromaticism, syncopation, and movement up and down the fingerboard, while retaining the integrity of the melody from Version 1.

TRACK 67

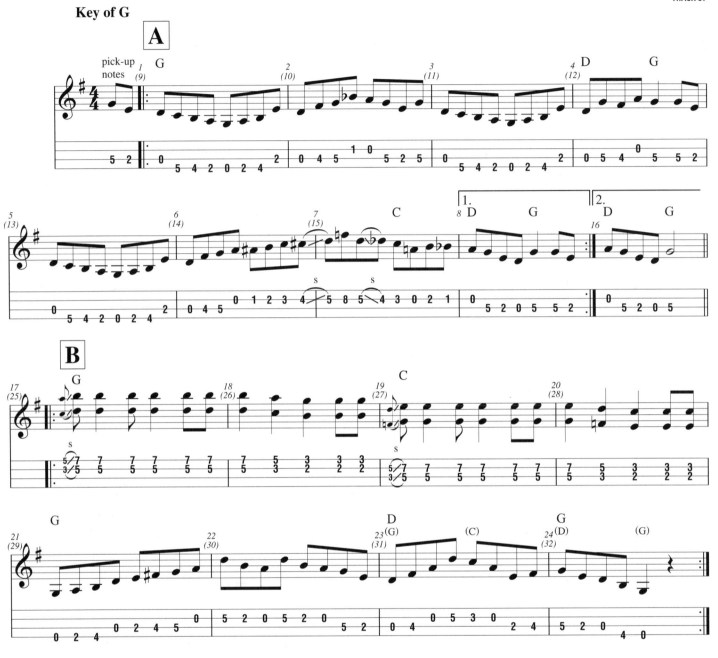

Alternate Licks by Section

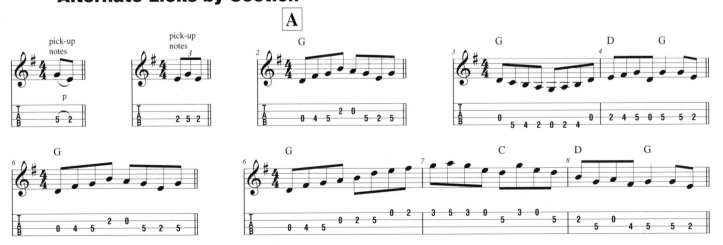

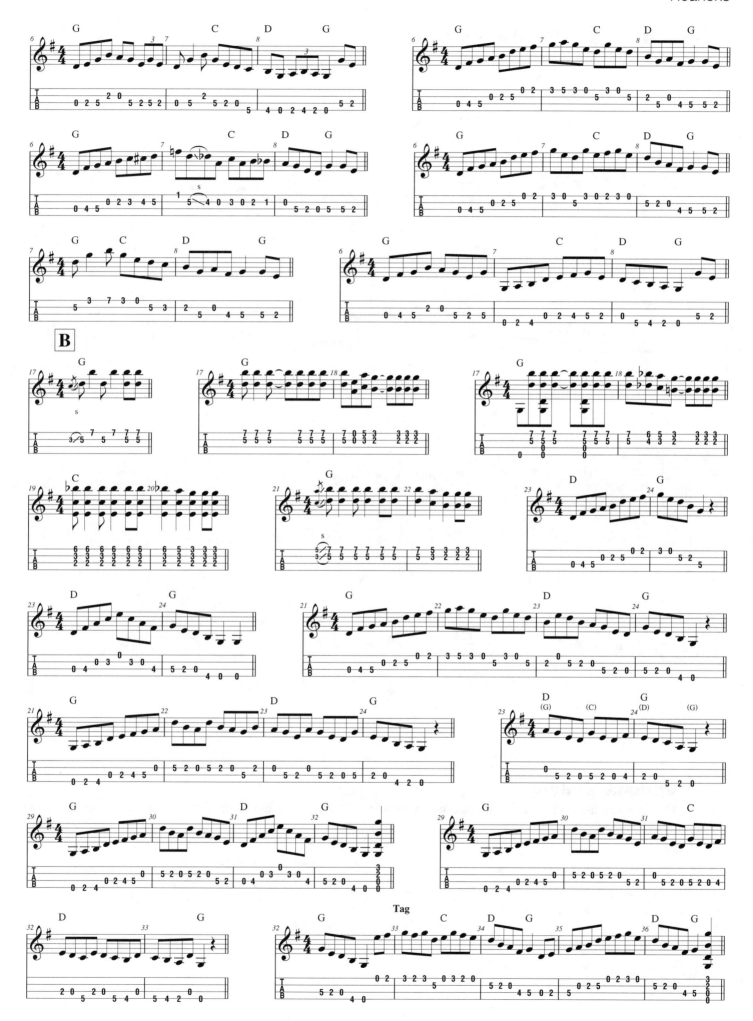

Version 3: Up-the-Neck

Here, Section A is played an octave higher than the previous versions, adding interest and unexpected tension to be resolved in Section B.

TRACK 68

Key of G

Optional Ending

This can be attached to any version starting on measure 32. Notice that it uses the exact same notes as the Intro for Version 1.

Alternate Licks for Section A

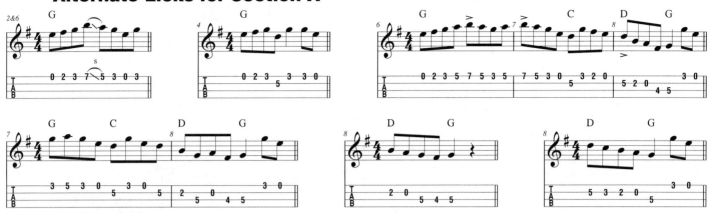

Alternate Section A

Three different options for Section A are offered below.

Alternate Licks for Section B

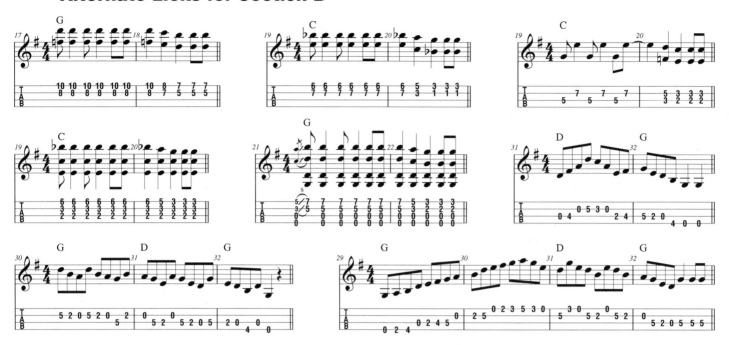

SLIPPED DISC

Music by Benny Goodman

Benjamin David Goodman was born the ninth of twelve children in 1909. Raised in Chicago, a strong music hub, Benny became almost an overnight prodigy on the clarinet. At the age of 16, he joined The Ben Pollack Orchestra and made his first professional recordings. In 1929, after his father passed away, Benny moved to New York City where he quickly became a very successful session musician. Around the same time, near the beginning of the Great Depression, Benny wisely purchased Fletcher Henderson's complete collection of charts. (Fletch played in New York's most popular African-American band during this time.) These charts, along with the musical style Benny was developing, paved the way to a style that earned Benny the title of "King of Swing."

His band's 1930s radio show, "Let's Dance," was highly popular from coast to coast. In 1935, the Goodman Band made a record that received rave reviews and went on tour. At the end of the tour, at the famous and huge Palomar Ballroom in Los Angeles, CA., Benny's new "swing" music, and the new "Jitterbug" dance created a new musical era for the United States—the swing era was born.

In 1957, Benny Goodman was accepted into the Jazz Hall of Fame. He passed away in 1986, but his music lives on.

"Slipped Disc" has one of those melodies that stays with you, and it is really fun to play on any instrument.

The first recording session of "Slipped Disc" was on February 4, 1945, and included the following musicians: Benny Goodman (clarinet), Red Norvo (vibraphone), Teddy Wilson (piano), Slam Stewart (bass), Mike Bryan (guitar), and Morey Feld (drums). They just didn't know what they were missing when they didn't include the mandolin! This tune seems as though it was written for the mandolin and is great fun to play. Among those who have recorded this tune on the mandolin are Jethro Burns and Peter Ostroushko.

Though originally in A♭, the following arrangements are in the key of G (a half step lower). These are based on the original clarinet composition. The first is played in the open-string area. It is easiest to learn it this way first. To add the left-hand slurs, simply move up the neck for measure 1–2 and 5–6.

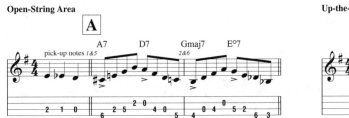

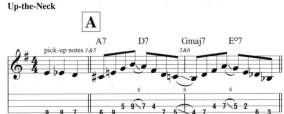

Version 2 stays with the basic melody from Version 1. The tablature for this version is written with measures 1–2 and 5–6 up the neck. Watch for the rests and pauses (silence). Above all, smile when you play this.

Version 1: Swing Melody

This arrangement is based on the original recording as played by Benny's clarinet. Instead of the basic I–IV–V progression, the chords work along the circle of fifths. Notice that each chord is the V chord of the next chord until the G chord (I chord) occurs—the home chord of the key. The back-up players usually interpret these chords as seventh chords. It is also interesting that the melody line does not address the chord's root, and that the first note of each eighth-note group moves down chromatically.

NOTE: The form of this tune consists of the A1 Section twice (only once on the audio) followed by Section B, then the A2 Section (basically Section A1) played once.

Also, in the alternate licks there is an optional ending. This can serve as a four-measure build-up to solos as well as an ending (obviously) that the band plays in *unison* (together). Keep this in mind when you're playing the forthcoming versions.

TRACK 69
(Played w/o repeats)

Key of G

Alternate Licks by Section

Version 2: Justifying the Title

Think about the title and you can often tell a story with your music. This is called *programmatic composing*, which is achieved by using musical techniques to enhance the audience's appreciation of the title. This arrangement does this by using sliding up the neck to "slip" into each new chord. This may take some practice because they occur on the off-beats, creating syncopation.

Key of G

Alternate Licks by Section

STARDUST

Words by Mitchell Parish   Music by Hoagy Carmichael

Hoagland Howard "Hoagy" Carmichael (November 22, 1899–December 27, 1981) was an American pianist who composed "Stardust," "Heart and Soul," "Georgia on My Mind," "(Up a) Lazy River," "Lazybones," and some of America's most recorded songs of all time.

"Stardust," a song about a song, has been reported as the #1 most recorded song in history. Artists who have recorded this tune include Glenn Miller, Louis Armstrong, Artie Shaw, Frank Sinatra, Dave Brubeck, Mel Tormé, Connie Francis, Harry Connick, Jr., Ella Fitzgerald, the Peanuts, the Shadows, Barry Manilow, John Coltrane, Rod Stewart, Willie Nelson, Johnny Mathis, Billy Ward and the Dominoes, Martin Denny, Ferrante and Teicher, Django Reinhardt, Tiny Tim, Billie Holiday, Dizzy Gillespie, Nat King Cole, and many more.

"Hoagy" was named Hoagland after a circus troupe, "the Hoaglands," who stayed at the Carmichael's home just before Hoagy was born. His mother, Lida, played accompaniment on the piano at silent movies. Hoagy began singing and playing the piano at age six. In high school, he enjoyed listening to ragtime pianists. During this time, he developed a friendship with Reg DuValle, a black bandleader and pianist, who taught him jazz piano improvisation. Hoagy earned his law degree in 1926 from the Indiana University School of Law, where he was a member of the Kappa Sigma fraternity. Through his college years, Hoagy entertained with the piano, earning the money to pay for his education. While in law school, he developed a strong friendship with a cornet player, Bix Beiderbecke, whose impressionistic and classical musical ideas had an influence over Hoagy's musical taste. He also began composing songs. In 1927, he passed the Indiana State Bar and joined a law firm, but by this time, he preferred to write and play music. Hoagy described his method for writing songs as, "You don't write melodies, you find them… if you find the beginning of a good song, and if your fingers do not stray, the melody should come out of hiding in a short time."

Hoagy composed and recorded "Star Dust" as a peppy, mid-tempo piano solo in 1927. In 1929, lyrics by Mitchell Parish were added, and the song was renamed "Stardust." In 1930, Isham Jones and his Orchestra recorded "Stardust" as a slow, sentimental ballad, which became a huge hit. To this day, the slower tempo is the standard for this beautiful song.

Verse:
And now the purple dusk of twilight time steals across the meadows of my heart
High up in the sky the little stars climb, always reminding me that we're apart
You wandered down the lane and far away, leaving me a song that will not die
Love is now the stardust of yesterday, the music of the years gone by

Chorus:
Sometimes I wonder why I spend the lonely night, dreaming of a song
The melody haunts my reverie, and I am once again with you
When our love was new and each kiss an inspiration
But that was long ago: now my consolation is in the stardust of a song

Beside a garden wall, when stars are bright you are in my arms
The nightingale tells his fairy tale of paradise, where roses grew
Tho' I dream in vain, in my heart it will remain
My star dust melody, the memory of love's refrain

Version 1: The Melody

This version is based on the piano score's melody played in C. This song's slow tempo calls for melancholy tremolo and an understated use of double stops. Adding unison notes via fretted and open strings effectively emphasizes the melody, however, these are optional.

NOTE: The chord symbols include jazz-style numerical suffixes, which add texture and color to the effect. These are also optional.

TRACK 70
(Played w/o repeats)

Version 1: The Melody *(cont.)*

Alternate Licks by Section

The triplet-based ideas can be heard on the original recordings.

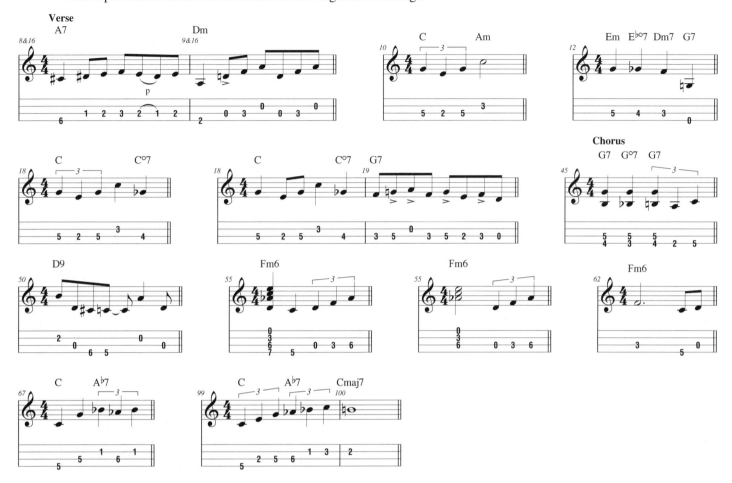

Version 2: Adding Harmony and Passing Tones

This arrangement builds on the previous version by adding optional harmony notes. The highest notes of these chords are the main melody, so play them only if you're uncomfortable with the fingerings. Passing notes are also included and optional. To omit the passing notes, sustain the note with an asterisk above it through the rest of the measure. Feel free to pick and choose which omissions sound best to you, but each note/chord adds to this song's beautiful fullness.

Key of C

Version 2: Adding Harmony and Passing Tones (cont.)

Alternate Endings

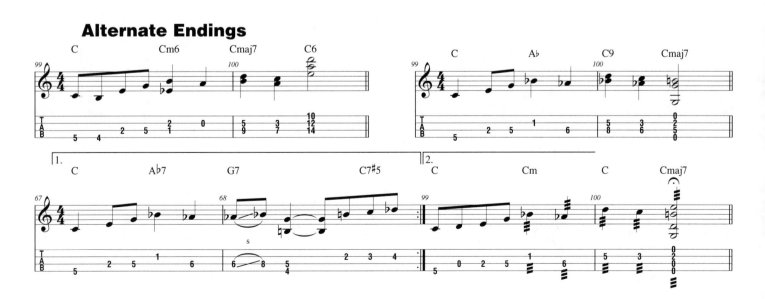

Alternate Licks by Section

194

Version 3: Key of F

The following arrangement is Version 1 transposed up a 4th to the key of F. Compare this version, measure by measure, to Version 1 to see these differences.

STUMBLING

Words and Music by Zez Confrey

"Stumbling" is a popular ragtime tune with a twist of classical and French impressionistic influence. The composer, Zez Confrey, called it a "foxtrot oddity." This tune has remained timeless and was even featured in the 1967 Julie Andrews film, *Thoroughly Modern Millie.* Zez Confrey also wrote the popular "Kitten on the Keys," "Dizzy Fingers," and other well-known ragtime tunes of the 1920s. His music combines a recognizable, tuneful melody with the syncopated rhythms of ragtime, which are peppy and engagingly light, reflective of a good, happy time. Zez Confrey's rags were highly popular in the 1920s, and virtually every band and pianist played his music.

Edward Elzear "Zez" Confrey (April 3, 1895–Nov 22, 1971) was born in Peru, Illinois, began piano lessons at an early age, and studied music at the Chicago Music College, run by Florenz Ziegfeld, Sr. His music is an interesting mixture of French impressionism influenced by Debussy and Ravel, along with the syncopated rhythms of ragtime. He was a pianist, composer, and bandleader who toured with the U.S. Navy in 1917. After World War I, Zez recorded over a hundred songs for the QRS Piano Roll Company. In addition, he played on the radio and recorded his piano music. In 1923, he published his first book, *Zez Confrey's Modern Course in Novelty Piano Playing*, which was highly popular and remained in print for over forty years.

"Stumbling" uses a classic form that was popular for many pop songs in the early part of the twentieth century. It begins with a Verse, which brings anticipation to the Chorus. Through the years, the Verses for many of these tunes have long been forgotten. Many musicians now perform these songs using the Chorus section only. The Verse is included in Version 3. To include it in Versions 1 or 2, simply insert the Verse between the Intro and Chorus, or omit the Intro.

Verse 1:
'Tention folks, speak of jokes, this is one on me
Took my gal to a dance at the Armory
Music played, dancers swayed, then we joined the crowd
I can't dance, took a chance, and right then we started

Chorus:
Stumbling all around, stumbling all around, stumbling all around so funny
Stumbling here and there, stumbling ev'rywhere, and I must declare
I stepped right on her toes, and when she bumped my nose, I fell
And when I rose, I felt ashamed and told her

That's the latest step, that's the latest step, that's the latest step, my honey
Notice all the pep, notice all the pep, notice all the pep
She said, "stop mumbling,_tho' you are stumbling
I like it just a little bit, just a little bit, quite a little bit"

Verse 2:
Young and small, short and tall, folks most ev'rywhere
Take a chance, do this dance, they think it's a bear
People rave, and they crave, just to do this step
Off they go, nice and slow, when the band starts playing

Chorus

Version 1: 1920s Classic Jazz/Swing

This is a fun-to-play, jazz-style tune. Notice that the chords revolve around the circle of fifths as V7 chords, which are dominant in quality. Each chord leads to the next until the song lands on G, the I chord. Adding the chord's 9th interval makes the jazz effect stronger.

Although originally written in the key of G, jazz musicians may transpose it down a whole step to F (see Versions 4–5). Additionally, to play it in the key of D, move every note one higher string over.

NOTE: Version 3 has the long-forgotten Verse. Transplanting it into any of the other versions works well.

TRACK 71

Version 1: 1920s Classic Jazz/Swing *(cont.)*

Alternate Licks

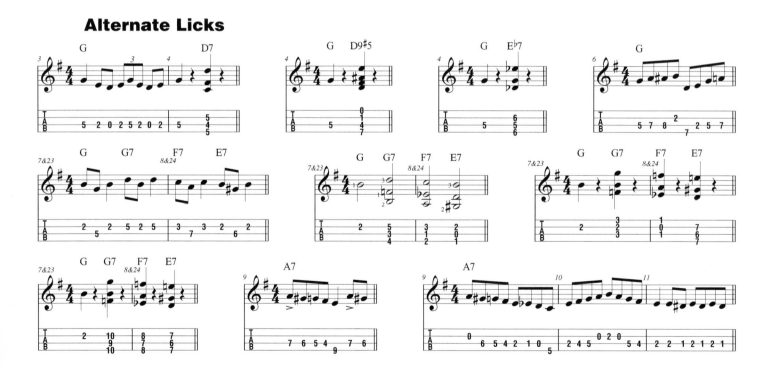

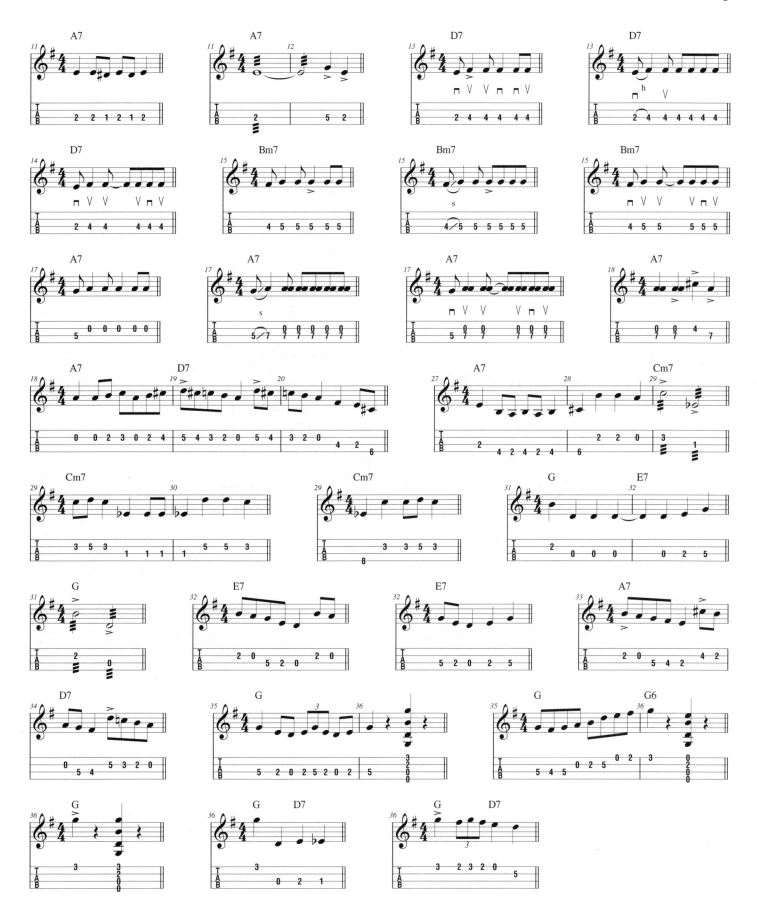

Version 2: Adding Chromaticism and Syncopation

This version will give your left-hand pinky a workout! However, if you're quick, you can use your index finger for two notes in a row. Also, see the alternate licks for measures 3 and 4 for a different effect. Keep in mind that this arrangement can be varied to suit your playing level as well as your musical taste.

TRACK 72

Key of G

Alternate Licks

Version 2: Alternate Licks (cont.)

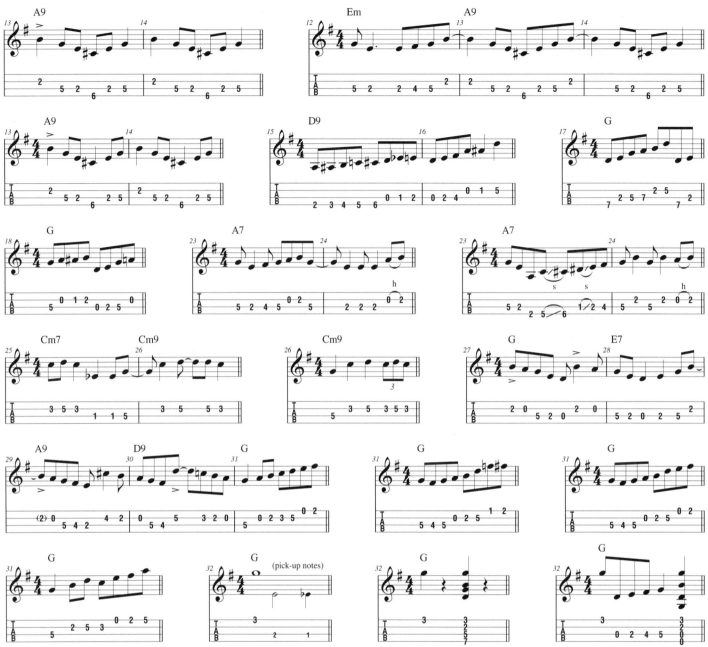

Version 3: Verse

This was the opening for the original score after the Intro. However, through the years, people have dropped the Verse, building their performances around the Chorus. Many songs written in the 1920s have been treated in this manner. For fun, ask the crowd to guess the song title by only playing the Verse. This also sounds nice with tremolo.

NOTE: The Verse follows the standard I–IV–V progression, as opposed to the circle of fifths in the Chorus section.

TRACK 73

Key of G

Verse

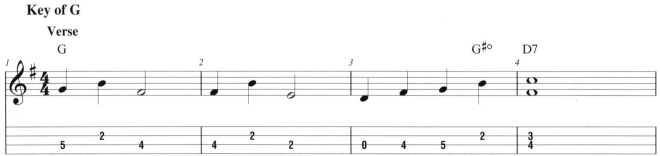

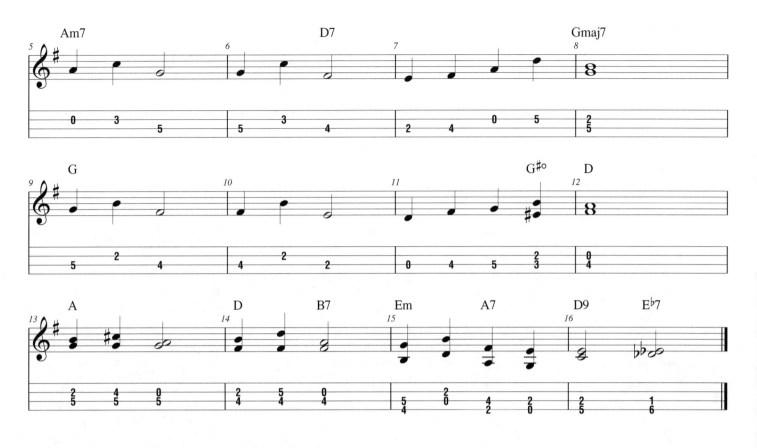

Alternate Licks

Alternate Verse with Syncopation

Instead of providing an exhaustive alternate licks section, below is a treatment closer to the original recording. These add more short-long syncopation which predominantly accents the up-beats.

Key of G

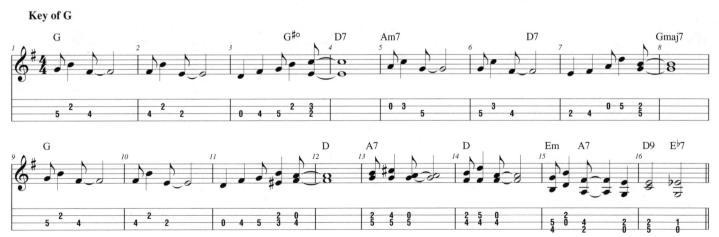

Version 4: Key of F

Played two frets lower than Versions 1 and 2, this version is often favored by jazz musicians. It also works well following a version in the key of G. To do so, simply play a C7 chord for measure 32 in the key of G to move smoothly into the key of F. C is a primary chord for both keys (serves as IV and V chord in keys of G and F, respectively), functioning as a *pivot chord* (a common chord to harmonies involved in a key change).

Alternate Licks

Version 5: Key of F

This corresponds to Version 2, which was written in the key of G. Bands usually play the F#°7–E♭7–D7 sequence in unison, stopping for rests, but here we don't. Transposing this version up a string yields the key of C, so explore that transposing possibility too.

Key of F

Alternate Licks

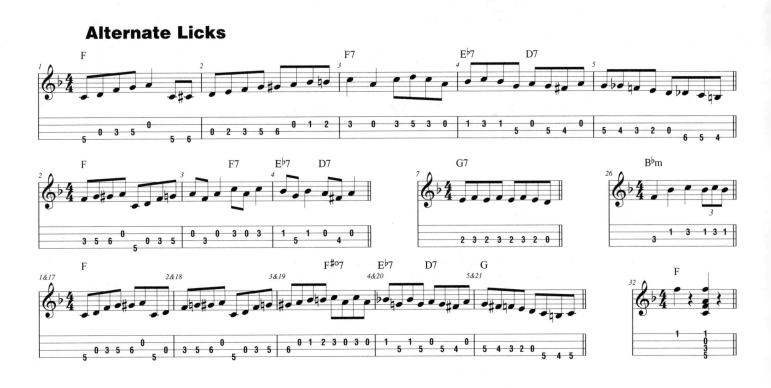

TENNESSEE WALTZ

Words and Music by Redd Stewart and Pee Wee King

"Tennessee Waltz" was co-written by Pee Wee King and Redd Stewart in 1948. The story is told that, while driving from Dallas, Texas to Nashville, Tennessee, they heard Bill Monroe's "Kentucky Waltz" on the radio. This inspired them to write a waltz to honor Tennessee. They started writing on the inside of a match box, completing the song by the time they arrived in Nashville. Like so many success stories, they had a difficult time finding someone to produce the tune. However, when Patti Page put this on side B of a hit single, it became a popular household tune all over America. In 1965, this became an official state song of Tennessee ("Rocky Top" shares this honor).

A *waltz* is a banjo song in 3/4 time. This means that each measure has six eighth notes, instead of the usual eight. The first version is played with eighth notes. The second version includes triplets. To compare the rhythms, the three notes in a triplet are to be played in the same amount of time as two eighth notes. If a rest occurs in a triplet, pause for that portion of the beat. Accent the first note of each measure. ONE–two–three, etc.

I was waltzin' with my darlin' to the Tennessee Waltz
When an old friend I happened to see
Introduced him to my loved one and while they were waltzing
My friend stole my sweetheart from me.

Chorus 1:
I remember the night and the Tennessee Waltz
'Cause I know just how much I have lost
Yes I lost my little darlin' the night they were playin'
The beautiful Tennessee Waltz

Now I wonder how a dance like the Tennessee Waltz
Could have broken my heart so complete
Well I couldn't blame my darlin', and who could help fallin'
In love with my darlin' so sweet

Chorus 2:
Well it must be the fault of the Tennessee Waltz
Wish I'd known just how much it would cost
But I didn't see it comin', it's all over but the cryin'
Blame it all on the Tennessee Waltz.

Version 1: Waltz in the Key of D

Musicians often improvise with the waltz rhythm in 3/4 time. Play this as you feel it while staying true to the basic melody. Add swing, blues, or jazz ideas from the alternate licks section to help in this area. Tremolo sounds great with this tune as well.

NOTE: To play in the key of G, move every note down one string and use the same fret numbers.

TRACK 74

Alternate Licks

Transposing from the Key of D to G

Key of D

Key of G

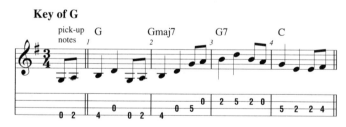

Version 2A: Harmony Notes

Try adding some tremolo once you get this arrangement under your fingers. Harmonizing the melody enhances the beauty of this tune. The melody note is the top note when harmony is added.

NOTE: The left-hand shapes should make the harmony easier to play.

TRACK 75

Key of D

Alternate Licks

Version 2B: Triplets and Harmony

This arrangement is based on Version 2A, offering different rhythms and ways to play harmony notes. Notice that the left-hand positions are different in several areas. When harmony notes are played, the melody is on the top, so retain that if you decide against playing the chords. Also, this version offers triplets to add interest and energy.

Key of D

Alternate Licks

Version 3: Triplets Up-the-Neck

See the introduction of "Tennessee Waltz" (page 210) for an explanation of triplets. For this version, hold two notes with the left hand at the same time like a chord, but pick the notes separately with the right hand. See "How Great Thou Art" (page 114) for more instruction in this style.

TRACK 76

Key of D

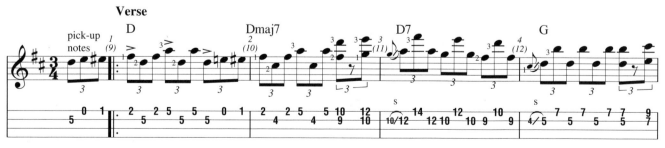

Alternate Licks

Version 3: Alternate Licks *(cont.)*

WHEEL HOSS

By Bill Monroe

From the time Bill Monroe and His Blue Grass Boys first recorded this tune on December 31, 1954, "Wheel Hoss" has been a popular Monroe fiddle tune. Numerous artists have recorded and helped to popularize this song among people who love the Monroe "sound," including Kenny Baker (Monroe's fiddler for many years), Ricky Skaggs (1985—won a Grammy award for best country instrumental performance with this song), Stoney Lonesome, Lilly Brothers, John Hickman, and numerous others. According to the liner notes of his *Bluegrass Instrumentals* album by Ralph Rinzler, a "wheel hoss" is a metaphor referring to a man who knew his job well and was doing it. This term technically refers to the two horses in the rear of a four-horse team. The "wheel hoss" are the two horses that take most of the stress from the heavily-loaded wagon and are responsible for accurately turning the wagon around the bends in the roads. To make the recording even more colorful so that the music without words is telling a story, Bill Monroe also makes the vocal sounds the wagon driver might make.

This tune was recorded about the same time "Roanoke" was originally recorded and with the same musicians playing the lead and back-up. In a tradition that began with the original recording and has continued today in most performances, the guitar ends each variation with the popular "Flatt" G run. The other instruments may stop for this to be played by the guitar alone, or they may accentuate this "signature lick" by also playing the standard "G lick" on their instruments. This occurs in measure 25 in the following arrangements.

Another interesting feature of "Wheel Hoss" is that Section A is played four times instead of the usual two times for standard fiddle tunes. Section B is played twice.

Measure 24 (just before the signature G lick) is a partial measure of 2/4 time. This is somewhat common in tunes from the mountains of Appalachia. To play this correctly, don't pause; keep going through the bar lines, and it will sound "right."

Sections A and B can be mixed and matched from version to version.

Version 1: Basic Melody

Looking for patterns while learning a new song helps in the quick digestion of the material. In this tune, notice that the same one-measure pattern—except measure 4—makes up the A section. Section B also offers the short-long rhythm pattern in measures 17 and 19.

TRACK 77

Key of G (Mixolydian)

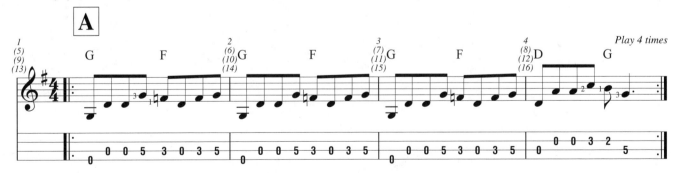

Version 1: Basic Melody (cont.)

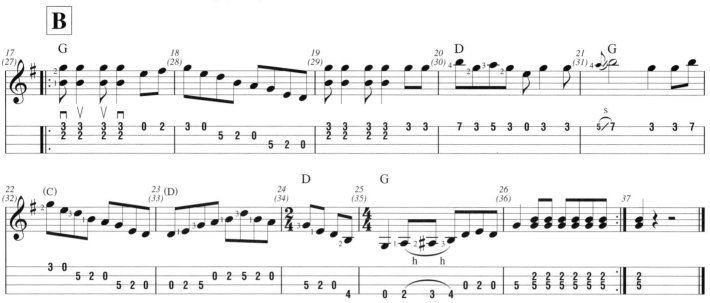

Alternate Licks by Section

These are popular licks recommended specifically for Version 1, but feel free to experiment with the others as well.

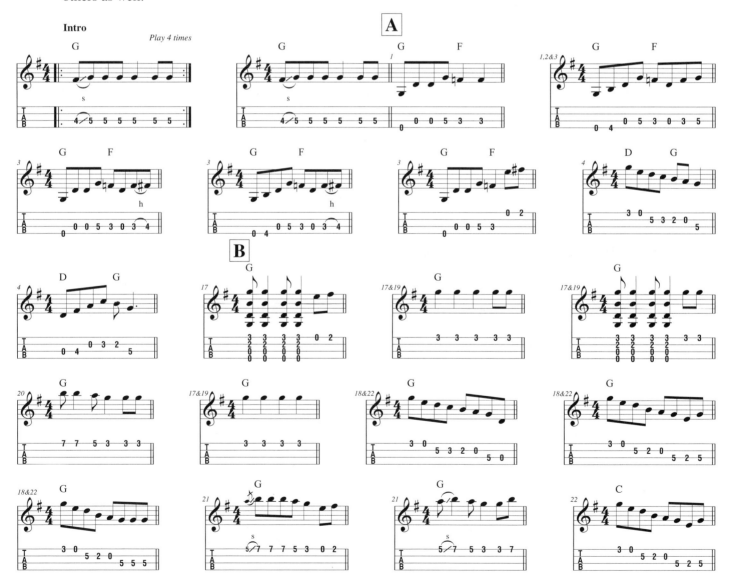

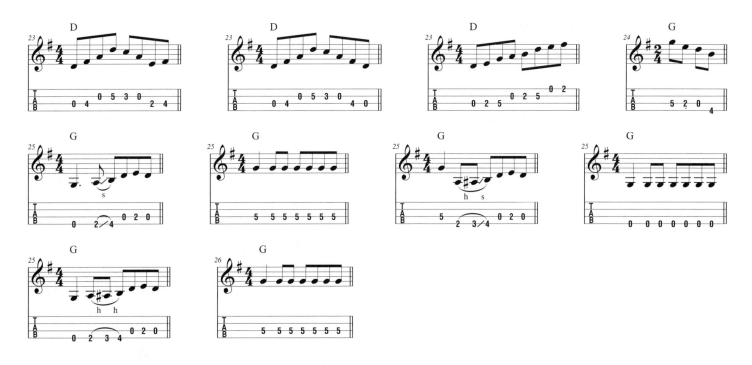

Version 2: Adding Scale Tones

Again, look for the patterns. Also, notice the subtle changes from Version 1, as in measure 3. This version is primarily based on tones from the G Mixolydian mode (G–A–B–C–D–E–F). Notice that the notes are from the G7 chord (G–B–D–F). The hammer-ons are optional.

TRACK 78

Key of G (Mixolydian)

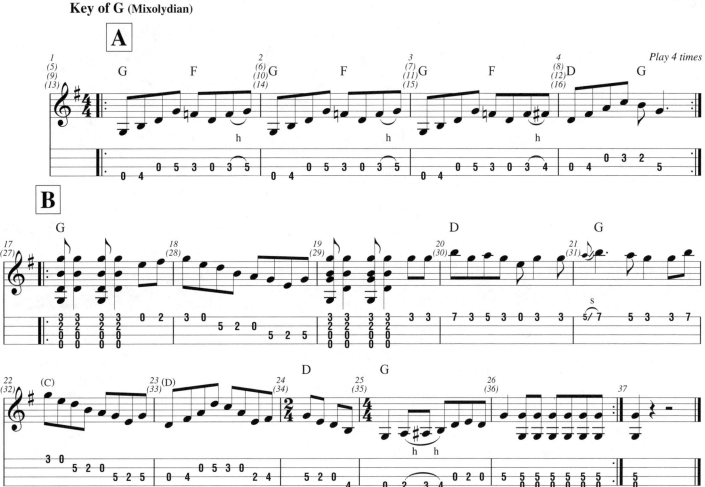

221

Alternate Licks by Section

Many of these licks use chromatic tones to create a bluesy, jazz-like flavor.

Version 3: Adding Chromatics, Slides, and Contemporary Sounds

This arrangement adds chromatic passing tones to add tension and a bluesy vibe. Because each section is repeated, the alternate licks provide interest and flair. This version uses all the tones of the *G Mixolydian mode* (the C major scale played from G to G), using the G and F chords as the main harmonic foundation.

TRACK 79

Key of G (Mixolydian)

Alternate Licks by Section

These ideas are exclusively applicable to this version. The next section has licks that can be used in any of the versions.

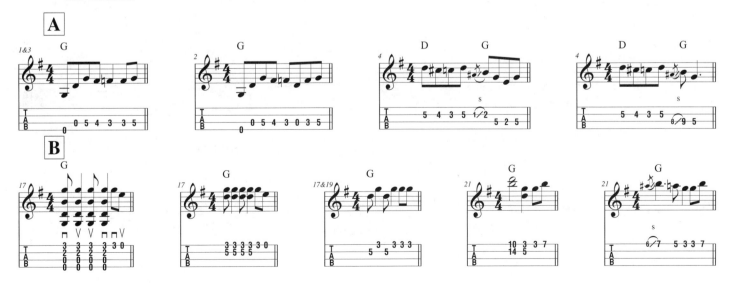

Version 3: Alternate Licks by Section (cont.)

Alternate Licks for All Versions by Section

Here we have licks that can be used for all versions, separated into sections.

YESTERDAY

Words and Music by John Lennon and Paul McCartney

"Yesterday" was written in 1965 and became one of Paul McCartney's best-known songs. Legend has it that this was so easy for him to write that he was afraid he might have heard it somewhere. He tested this by playing it for many people before he finally recorded it. No one recognized the tune or the words. Now? "Yesterday" is recognized as a Beatles tune by people of all ages. It has been recorded and promoted an incredible number of times by artists throughout the following years.

The Beatles were the world's favorite rock group in the 1960s. Their lyrics were about love, social criticisms, silly ideas, symbolism ballads, and just about anything they felt like writing about. Their musical sound was also more complex than the rock 'n' roll era of the 1950s, when people were used to listening to songs based primarily upon I–IV–V and I–vi–IV–V chord progressions, yet their music flowed smoothly.

"Yesterday" is an excellent example of an ingenious Beatles chord progression. This a natural and fun tune to play on the mandolin in the key of F.

The triplets used in Version 3 are quarter-note triplets. (These were also used in "Autumn Leaves" [Version 3] and for the alternate licks in "El Cumbanchero.")

Tri - po - let   Tri - po - let

Yesterday, all my troubles seemed so far away
Now it looks as though they're here to stay
Oh I believe in yesterday

Suddenly, I'm not half the man I used to be
There's a shadow hanging over me
Oh yesterday came suddenly

Chorus:
Why she had to go, I don't know, she wouldn't say
I said something wrong, now I long for yesterday

Yesterday, love was such an easy game to play
Now I need a place to hide away
Oh I believe in yesterday

Chorus

Yesterday, love was such an easy game to play
Now I need a place to hide away
Oh I believe in yesterday

Version 1: Melody with Tremolo

This version is very effective if performed with tremolo throughout. Work up to this by learning the melody first. Remember to hold the sustained notes the correct number of beats. Once you feel the rhythm, use it. The form of this song, after the Intro, consists of the Verse twice, Chorus, and the Verse again to the Coda. To shorten the performance, play the Verse once and skip directly to the Coda. On the audio, the Intro and repeats aren't played.

TRACK 80
(Played w/o repeats or Intro)

Key of F

Version 1: Melody with Tremolo *(cont.)*

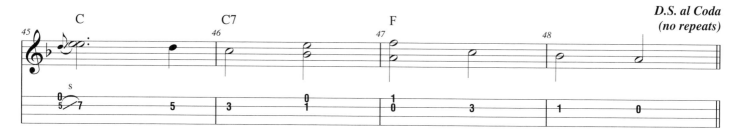

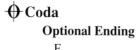

Alternate Licks by Section

Version 2: Adding Harmony Notes

This arrangement uses Version 1 as a foundation for the harmony notes. Use the alternate licks to take full advantage of this effect by using the corresponding measure numbers. As with other songs, the harmony notes are optional. The melody is the top note (highest pitched) in each double stop or chord.

Key of F

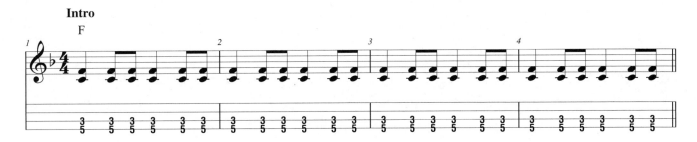

Version 2: Adding Harmony Notes (cont.)

Coda

Optional Ending

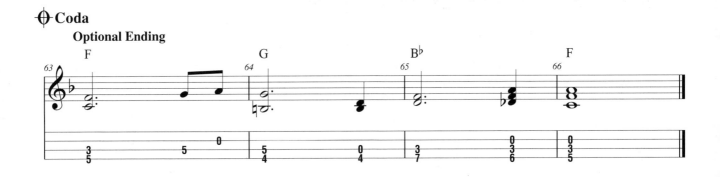

Alternate Licks by Section

Version 3: Improvising Up-the-Neck

This version was originally another alternate licks section, but when I combined them, they turned out to be a great-sounding variation. Some points of interest are measures 13–14 using triplets and measures 33–35, which use the interval of an *octave* (same note eight scale steps apart) to play the melody. This requires a bit of a stretch, but it's worth the effort for the contemporary sound.

TRACK 81
(Played w/o repeats or Intro)

Alternate Licks by Section

Verse

Chorus

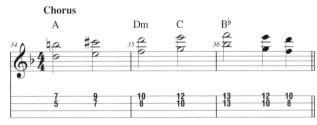 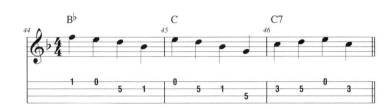

Version 4: Bluegrass Style

This version is meant to be played at a faster tempo and involves playing a combination of tremolo and bluegrass scale-style runs.

TRACK 82
(Played w/o repeats
or Intro)

Key of F

Intro

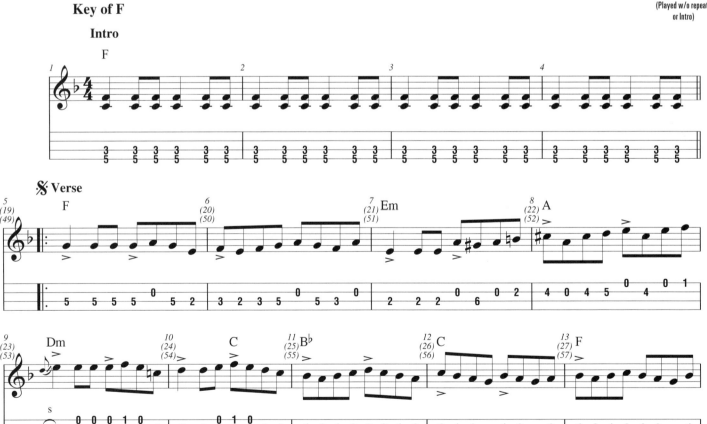

Alternate Licks by Section

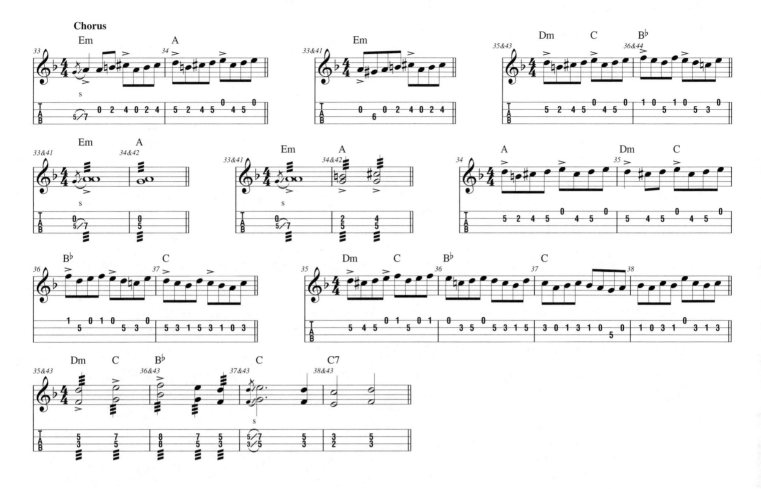

YOU ARE MY SUNSHINE

Words and Music by Jimmie Davis

One of the world's most recognized songs of all time, "You Are My Sunshine" has been translated into thirty plus languages. King George VI of England is said to have declared this his favorite tune. Like so many other classic tunes, this tune is also an official state song (Louisiana).

Jimmie Davis (1899–2000), the oldest of eleven children, grew up in a two-bedroom house. He earned a master's degree from LSU, where he served as a history professor. His interest in politics and in recording music began about the same time. In 1935, "Nobody's Darling but Mine" became his first major hit, followed by "It Makes No Difference Now." In Chicago, he recorded "You Are My Sunshine," which quickly became known worldwide. Continuing his political career, in 1944, Jimmie was elected governor of Louisiana. The state treasury had a surplus when he left office, and he had accomplished this without raising taxes. In the 1950s, he turned to gospel music and wrote some great hits, such as "Honey in the Rock" (a favorite Lewis family tune). In the 1960s, the state was having problems, and Jimmie was once again elected governor. When he left office, the problems had once again been successfully addressed without a tax increase.

Jimmie Davis was inducted in the Country Music Hall of Fame in 1972 and into the Gospel Music Hall of Fame in 1997. All honors aside, he will forever be remembered for writing a song that is enjoyed and passed down in families from generation to generation.

The versions for the mandolin are presented in the order of difficulty. The last arrangement uses crosspicking in the key of D. This is a challenging and effective picking style that really fits the tune.

The other night, dear, as I lay sleeping
I dreamed I held you in my arms
When I awoke, dear, I was mistaken
And I hung my head and cried.

Chorus:
You are my sunshine, my only sunshine
You make me happy when skies are grey
You'll never know dear, how much I love you
Please don't take my sunshine away.

I'll always love you and make you happy
If you will only say the same
But if you leave me to love another
You'll regret it all some day

Chorus

You told me once, dear, you really loved me
And no one else could come between
But now you've left me and love another
You have shattered all my dreams

Chorus

Version 1: Melody with Tremolo

This tune has a very identifiable melody, so establishing it the first time you play through it is very important. The following arrangement, hopefully, serves this purpose. If you stay with the beat and play the tremolo as you feel it, your version can't help but be a success. See the alternate licks to include the open A string as an easy-to-add harmony note. To play in the key of A, simply play the same fret positions over on the adjacent higher string.

TRACK 83
(Played w/o repeats)

Key of D

Alternate Licks

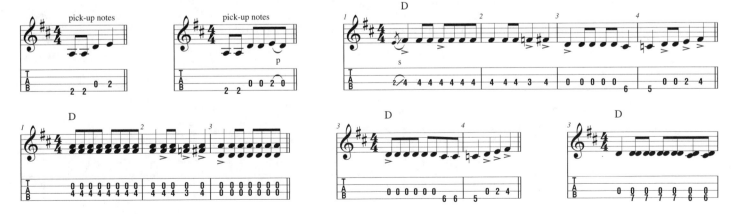

Version 1: Alternate Licks *(cont.)*

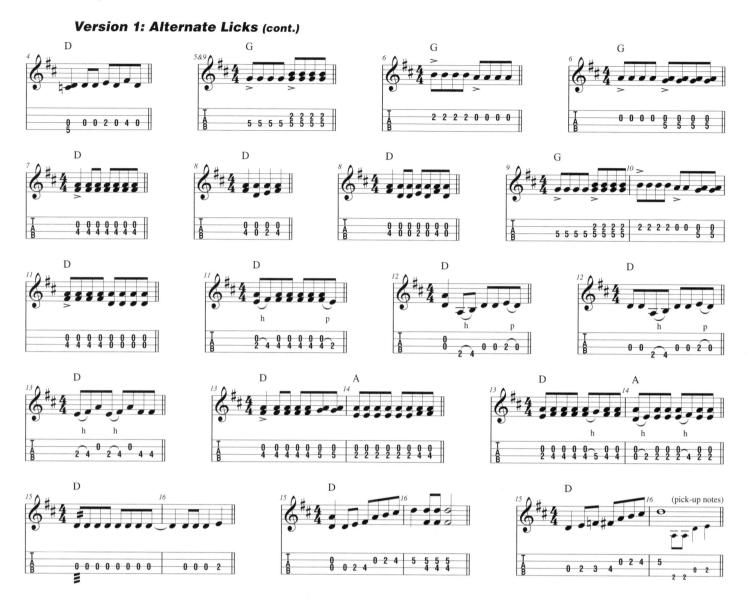

Version 2: Adding Harmony

The A string makes an effective harmony note for most of the melody notes in the key of D. Additional harmony notes are used based on the back-up chord being played. As said before, the melody is on the bottom and add tremolo at your own discretion. The melody for both the Verse and Chorus are the same, but measure 6 uses slightly different rhythmic placement (see alternate measure 6 for the Chorus).

NOTE: To transpose to the key of G or A, play each on the adjacent string that is lower and higher in pitch, respectively.

TRACK 84
(Played w/o repeats)

Key of D

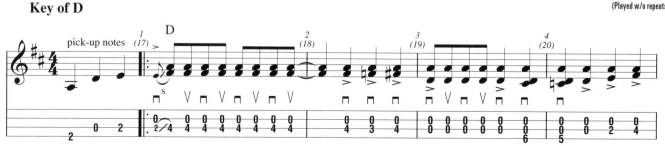

Alternate Licks

Version 2: Alternate Licks *(cont.)*

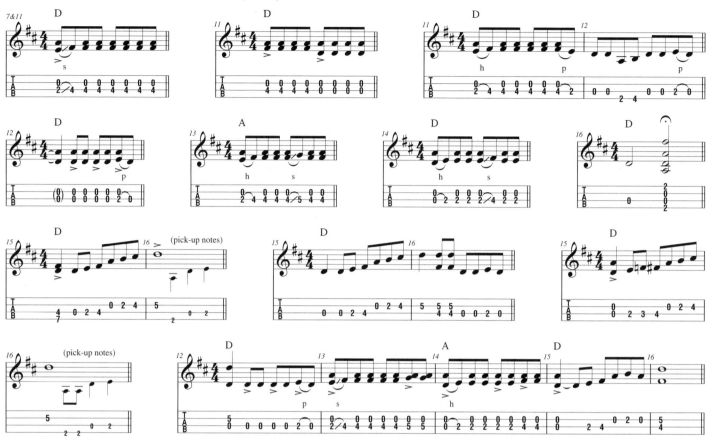

Version 3: Adding Bluegrass Licks

For fun, bluegrass licks are substituted by chord in measures 5–12. (Remember the G lick from "Wheel Hoss"?) This lick is also a *pattern* that can be played for any chord. Notice that the left-hand fingering pattern for the G lick in measure 5 is also used for the D lick in measure 7, but up one string.

TRACK 85
(Played w/o repeats)

Key of D

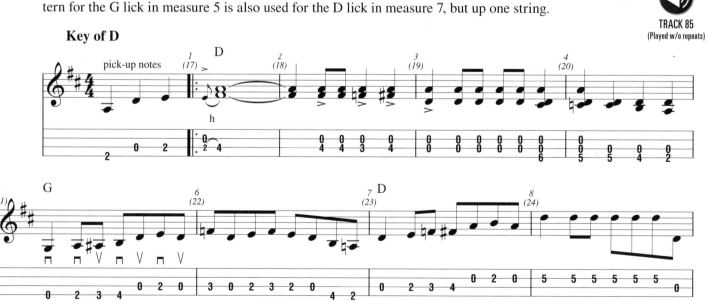

Alternate Licks

Combine a sequence from measures 4–16 from the alternate licks to form a new version.

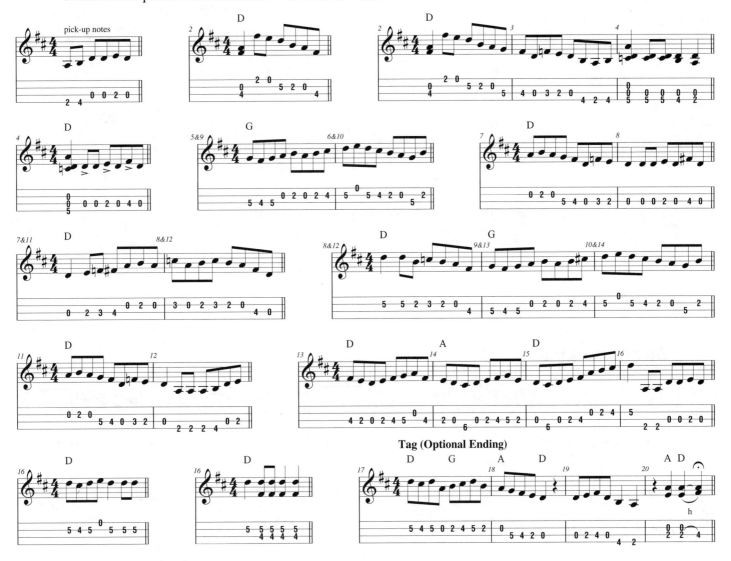

Version 4: Substituting Licks

This version builds on Version 3 by changing the licks for the G and D chords in measures 5–14 to take on a stronger bluegrass effect, without adding difficulty. To enhance this, play the alternate measures for the pick-up notes through measure 4.

TRACK 86
(Played w/o repeats)

Key of D

Alternate Licks

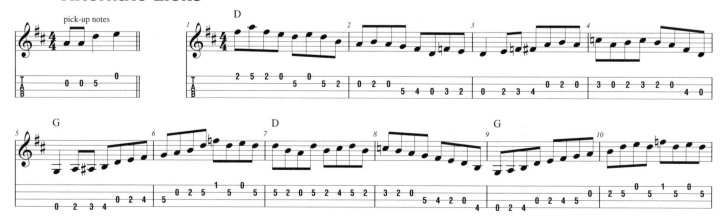

Version 5: Up-the-Neck Using Only Two Strings

When looking at the tablature, the higher positions may be intimidating. However, notice that only two strings are used to play the song, so the left-hand fingering is fairly simple.

TRACK 87
(Played w/o repeats)

Key of D

Alternate Licks

Along with the other alternate licks, I've included fingerings for Version 5 that stay in the open-string area.

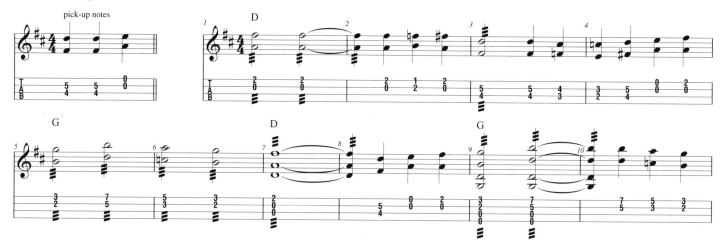

Version 6: Crosspicking

Crosspicking is a technique that involves using the same pick direction for attacks on adjacent strings. Here, the melody follows along one string with two open strings serving as a drone-style harmony. Check out the tablature for the logistics and follow the picking suggestions closely (down–up–up). Since down-strokes are stronger, this helps emphasize the melody note.

NOTE: Play measure 1 with the open strings first, as this is the basic eight-note pattern. Notice the same pattern is used almost exclusively until the end.

TRACK 88
(Played w/o repeats)

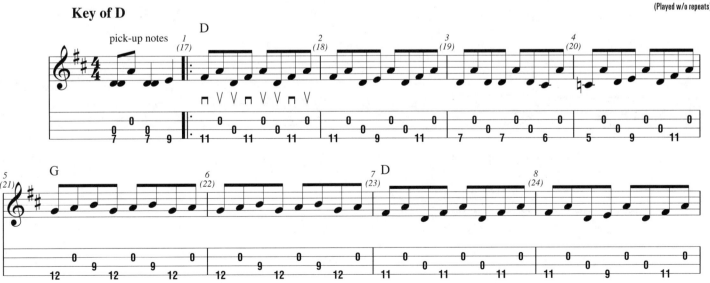

Version 6: Crosspicking *(cont.)*

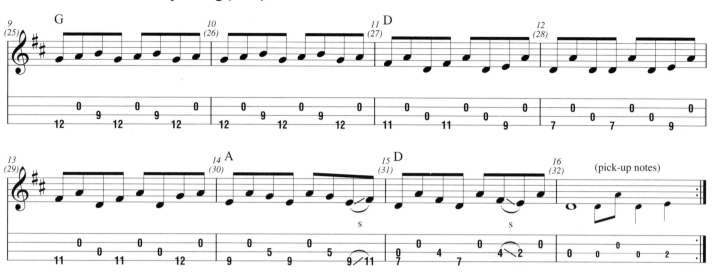

Alternate Licks

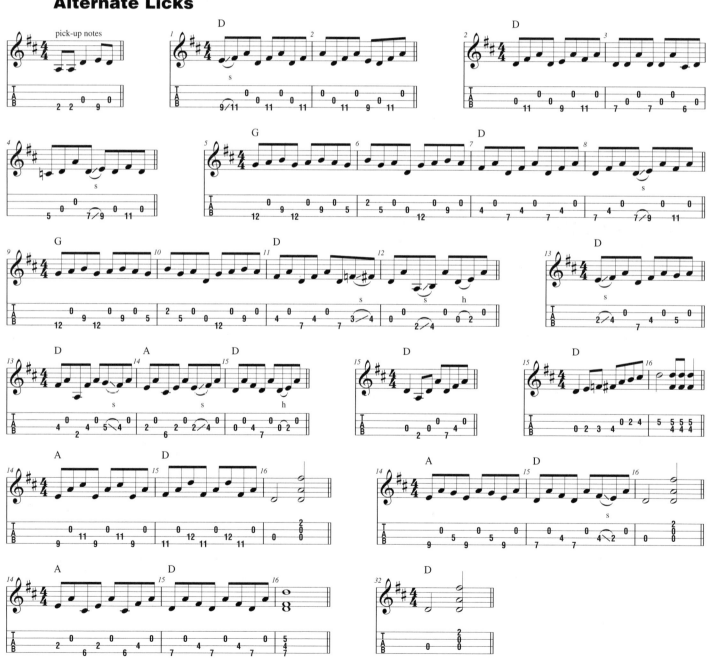